Praise for *They Saw Through God's Eyes*

"Seeing the world as God sees it must be one of the most freeing and humbling ways to live! This book inspires us to try—and it uses the example of our Blessed Mother and the saints to prove we too can make that our goal."
—Rachel Balducci, author of *Overcomitted: Cut Chaos and Find Balance*

"There's no other meaning, reason, or purpose to our lives than to become a saint—to be in heaven with God for all eternity. This is a book to show us that's possible, for you and for me."
—Jon Leonetti, author of *Life, Liberty, and the Pursuit of Holiness*

"In *They Saw Through God's Eyes*, Deacon Matt Halbach challenges us to see 'as God sees.' In this deceptively simple but deeply thought-provoking book, Deacon Halbach details the lives of saints then parallels their stories to his ʳ ᵉal-life encounters with modern saints-in-the-mak⸍ ˎ reflection questions and a prayer rounding ᵖ we too are inspired to strive for sanc⸍ through God's eyes: as gifts to be ˏd offered back to the Lord."
—Karen Edmisten, author of *The ⸍ ⸍ of Cath-olic Days: A Guide to Feasts, Saints, ⸍ ⸍, and Seasons*

"Eye-opening and heartwarming! Deacon Matthew Halbach has given us an inspiring way of looking at our lives and the world around us—and seeing saints among us. *They Saw Through God's Eyes* offers compelling profiles of saints we know—and future saints you will want to know!—who bring meaning and purpose to our world today. RCIA groups, students, and just curious Catholics will want to add this to their library."
—Deacon Greg Kandra, blogger and author of *The Busy Person's Guide to Prayer*

"Faith is a way of seeing. This little book will open the eyes of your heart to discover how God is alive and well and living in your life as God has always done through those whom we call saints. They are people like you and me—no different from you and me—who discovered that by letting Jesus be the center of their lives they could become who they really are in God's eyes. I am so grateful to Deacon Matt for opening the door on this 'God's eye view' of my life and yours. Read and become who you are."
—Bishop Edward Scharfenberger, Diocese of Albany

"What a wonderful set of meditations! Deacon Matt has taken some of our holiest and most revered saints and brought them down to earth for us—all so that we can capture their unique vision of God and let that vision fill our hearts and minds. He has opened up the lives of twelve revered saints and revealed the unique, Spirit-inspired way each of them

met the Lord. And not only that, but he shows us the way to have that same encounter ourselves. What an achievement!"
—Leo Zanchettin, author of *Encountering the Lord in the Gospel of Mark*

They Saw Through
God's Eyes

An Invitation from Mary and the Saints

Deacon Matthew Halbach

the**WORD**
among us®
press

Published by The Word Among Us Press
7115 Guilford Drive, Suite 100
Frederick, Maryland 21704
wau.org

25 24 23 22 21   1 2 3 4 5

ISBN: 978-1-59325-606-7
eISBN: 978-1-59325-607-4

Design by Suzanne Earl

Made and printed in the United States of America

Library of Congress Control Number: 2022902786

Contents

A Note to the Reader

As Catholics, we are always on the lookout for God's presence and purpose in our life. Seeing life through the lens of faith nourishes us and inspires us to live up to our full potential and to pursue a life of holiness. Life, after all, is a gift. At least, that's how God sees it. But do you see it this way?

In this book, I hope not only to help you see your life as a gift from God but also to help you see it, in some measure, as God sees it. That might sound overpromising. How can we possibly see as God sees? But the saints and everyday saints-in-the making demonstrate that this is, in fact, possible. Through the Church, Scripture, prayer, the sacraments, and any number of ways, God reveals the meaning of life and how he wants us to live this gift.

The people I discuss in the following pages discovered for themselves the truth of how God sees things. That insight and knowledge transformed them. They saw what God wanted for them—his will for them—and conformed themselves to that, no matter the cost. They had what I like to think of as a God's-eye view of things.

I hope this book helps you examine your own life and see it as God sees it. Each chapter includes information about a saint and a modern example of someone who has come to see God's truth in their own life. Questions for reflection and a prayer round out every chapter, helping you ponder the material from the perspective of your life circumstances. Read it cover-to-cover, if you choose, or dip into it in no particular order. Each chapter stands alone as a possible gateway into a God's-eye view of your life.

My prayer is that you will allow God to open the eyes of your heart, "that you may know what is the hope that belongs to his call, what are the riches of glory in his inheritance among the holy ones, and what is the surpassing greatness of his power for us who believe" (Ephesians 1:18-19). May you come to appreciate and celebrate your life as God does.

CHAPTER 1

Mary, Mother of God

Seeing the Glory of God
in Our Lowliness

There is nothing immediately attractive about the word "lowliness." It brings to mind the word "insignificance"—an unappealing word as well. But from a biblical standpoint, holiness and lowliness go hand in hand. God raising up the lowly and bringing down the mighty is a frequent theme throughout the Old and New Testaments (see 1 Samuel 2:7; 2 Samuel 22:28; Job 5:11-16; 12:19; Psalm 147:6; Sirach 10:14; Luke 1:52; James 4:6; 1 Peter 5:5).

As the priest brings his hands down over the simple gifts of bread and wine in the act of consecration, so God sends down his Spirit to consecrate (set apart) people for his service. Those who are lowly are particularly open to receiving the call and blessing of God. As the Beatitudes teach, "Blessed are the poor in spirit, for theirs is the kingdom of heaven," and, "Blessed are the meek, for they shall inherit the earth" (Matthew 5:3, 5, RSVCE).

Mary had a heart completely open to God's plan—even when that plan seemed impossible. Her openness prepared the way for God to consecrate and raise her up to be mother of God and therefore mother of the Church. She is the perfect example of *holy lowliness*.

Lowliness: Humble Trust That We Are Loved

At the annunciation (Luke 1:26-38), the angel Gabriel came to a Jewish peasant announcing God's plan of salvation. While the annunciation has been romanticized quite a bit, Scripture makes it clear that Mary found the experience troubling (29-30) and confusing (34). None of these emotions take away from the supernatural nature of the event or from Mary's dignity as the chosen vessel of the Lord. Gabriel attests to Mary's unique blessedness within God's plan at the very beginning of his greeting, when he proclaims her to be highly favored—"full of grace" (28, RSVCE).

After hearing that God has chosen to save his people through a child whom she will conceive in her womb by the power of the Spirit, Mary responds with profound humility and trust: "May it be done to me according to your word" (Luke 1:38). Because Mary chose to embrace her role as the Lord's *handmaid* (48), the world is forever changed.

Lowliness Allows Us to Recognize God's Plan in Our Lives

Holy lowliness keeps the focus off us, so that we are better able to discern the unfolding of God's saving plan. Mary demonstrated this aspect of lowliness at the visitation, when her cousin Elizabeth—and Elizabeth's son, John—recognized Mary's consecration by God (see Luke 1:39-56). Elizabeth proclaimed Mary blessed among women and the child in Mary's womb blessed as well (42). At the same moment that Elizabeth recognized Mary as the mother of her Lord, Elizabeth's unborn son, in agreement, leapt in the womb (43-44). Mary, in her humility, could receive these acclamations.

Elizabeth's and John's recognition of Mary's role in God's saving plan released in her a truth that perhaps had been growing inside her from the time of her Immaculate Conception: namely, that God had chosen her to be "blessed among women" (42), beyond all merit and understanding. In response to Elizabeth and John, Mary exclaimed:

> My soul proclaims the greatness of the Lord;
>> my spirit rejoices in God my savior.
> For he has looked upon his handmaid's lowliness;
>> behold, from now on will all ages call me blessed.
> (Luke 1:46-48)

The word "proclaims" in verse 46 is sometimes translated "magnifies," with roots in the Latin *magnificare* (see

Luke 1:46, RSVCE). The Magnificat is the traditional title of Mary's proclamation.

A Posture of Obedience

We are lowly, in a holy sense, when we are willing to obey God and those he has placed in authority. (Not everyone in authority has been placed there by God!) At the wedding feast at Cana, the wedding party runs out of wine (see John 2:1-12). Mary speaks to Jesus, confident that he can do something about it. After speaking with her son, Mary tells the servers, "Do whatever he tells you" (5). Jesus tells the servers to fill the six stone jars with water. They obey. When they serve the liquid from the jars, it has become wine.

Someone who is lowly embraces a posture of obedience, not a blind obedience but one built on trust. Mary trusts her son. She knows he is the promised Messiah who has come to deliver Israel. Similarly, Jesus shows his lowliness by responding to his mother's request for help. When the servers obey Mary's command to listen to her son, they too demonstrate an attitude of lowliness, trusting Mary.

Lowliness Allows Us to Put the Needs of Others before Our Own

After Jesus' trial, many of the apostles fled for fear of Roman or Jewish reprisal. They were thinking about their own lives and the lives of their families. But not Mary; she didn't flee. At the crucifixion, we find her by her son's side, supporting him with her presence and her prayers (see John 19:25-27). She couldn't be anywhere but at her son's side as he surrendered his spirit to the Father.

Mary placed her entire life at the service of Jesus, loving him and placing his needs before hers. Various Church Fathers compared her to the moon: just as the moon's light is only the reflection of the sun's, Mary didn't produce her own light but reflected the light of her son. Mary always put Jesus first.

Magnifying the Lord

While teaching RCIA, I met a woman whom, for anonymity's sake, we'll call Deb. It took very little convincing to bring Deb into the Catholic faith. She was ready to be Catholic from day one.

One thing I noticed about Deb was her seemingly total lack of pride. When I paid her a compliment, she'd accept it and—unlike me!—not fish for more. She hardly talked about herself, and when she did, it was always in reference to God or her family. She reflected their light, not her own.

This isn't to suggest that Deb thought little of herself. Rather there was a holy lowliness about her that came from her confidence in God and in her family's love for her. Knowing she was loved, she didn't need to draw attention to herself. She was genuinely invested in others, and that made her a joy to be around.

Deb was always putting others first. Before each RCIA session, she'd ask if I needed anything copied or stapled. She frequently volunteered to bring snacks for our group. As the RCIA continued, her influence spread to the parish. She got involved in parish activities, both as a participant and as a volunteer. By the end of RCIA, Deb was coordinating an annual fun run for vocations at our parish—her own idea. The money earned from the run went to support the diocesan seminary fund.

Sadly, just one year after becoming Catholic, Deb was diagnosed with terminal lung cancer. She was in her early forties and had never smoked in her life, so the diagnosis was a shock. She began chemotherapy, lost her hair, and grew very sick and weak. After a few months, the doctors determined that continuing the chemo would only buy her a little time, so she declined further treatment.

Instead of staying at home and waiting for death, Deb became even more active in the parish. She attended daily Mass and stayed afterward to visit with people and pray with them. She also started a women's group, something she had wanted to do since the beginning of RCIA. The meetings included a study of exemplary and heroic women of the Bible, a Rosary, and a social hour, all of which Deb organized and facilitated. Deb's gift for supporting others and building them up came naturally to her. Everyone who met her came away a better person.

Deb organized a final fun run for vocations before her death. To everybody's astonishment, she participated in the run. Her family and fellow parishioners helped her make the entire 6.2 miles (a 10K).

It seemed as if the entire parish turned out for Deb's funeral. The church was packed with people who wanted to pay their respects to a woman who had said and done little to promote herself and, because of this, magnified the Lord brightly in our parish. I will never forget her.

FOR REFLECTION

1. Do you think you're special to God, that he has a plan for you? Consider the impact that plan has had on you so far. Not sure he has a plan? Talk with a priest or spiritual director to begin to explore ways you can open yourself to that truth.

2. Holy lowliness is rooted in our humble acceptance of God's love for us and in our appreciation of his greatness. How do you practice an appreciation for God's greatness as you go about your life each day?

3. From the cross, Jesus gave Mary to the Church. Has Mary been a gift in your life? If so, how? If not, ask her to help you grow in appreciation of her maternal care for you.

FOR PRAYER

Mary, because of your lowliness, you were able to embrace the impossible promise of God: that he would one day send Israel a savior, born of a virgin (see Isaiah 7:14). You were the vessel of that promise. Help me humbly embrace my great need for God and thereby open myself up to his great love for me. Amen.

CHAPTER 2

Mary Magdalene

Seeing Our Need for
Spiritual Transformation

Society places a strong emphasis on the ongoing work of personal transformation. Consider all the talk and print about exercise, nutrition, therapy, meditation, and the countless things we do to manage our physical and mental health. But what about our spiritual health? How do we take care of that? How do we maintain our focus on spiritual transformation?

God created us both body and soul; therefore the health of our body impacts the health of our soul, and the health of our soul—our spirit—impacts the health of our body. It's a two-way street. Scripture tells us that we are made in God's "image" and "likeness," but sin keeps us from experiencing the fullness and abundance God has promised us (see Genesis 1:26; John 10:10).

Because sin has so disoriented us—taken us off track—God needs to bring us back to the path of loving relationship with him. This reorientation can happen subtly, over time, or it can happen dramatically, arriving in radical fashion. In either case, it saves us from sin and death and prepares us for eternal life in heaven. And in either case, it is Jesus who effects the transformation.

St. Mary Magdalene experienced a radical spiritual transformation when she encountered Jesus. The Gospels tell us that Jesus cast out seven demons from Mary (see Mark 16:9; Luke 8:2) and that she was his disciple from that point on. What a beginning to her journey of faith!

For most of us, spiritual transformation is far less earthshaking. It might come in the quiet hush of the confessional or during our private prayer time. Nevertheless, Mary Magdalene reminds us that spiritual transformation always happens when we encounter Jesus Christ, accept his love for us, and allow that love to change us. Mary's encounter with Jesus eventually transformed her into what Pope Francis described as "the *Apostle of the new and greatest hope*."[1]

From Outcast to Disciple

Mary was from Magdala (hence she is called Magdalene), a town on the west shore of the Sea of Galilee. Not much is known of Mary's early life. Even the nonbiblical apocryphal sources are silent about the time in Mary's life before she became a disciple of Jesus.

Further, there are a lot of Marys in the New Testament, and sometimes it's difficult to tell which Mary is being referred to in a particular passage. Consequently there has been longstanding confusion about what other things Mary Magdalene did or didn't do. For example, in the Western Church, from the time of Pope Gregory I (AD 591) to Pope Paul VI (1969), Mary Magdalene was identified as the "sinful woman" who anointed Jesus' feet with her tears and dried them with her hair (Luke 7:37). This led to her misidentification as a prostitute, a term Scripture never applies to her.

Mary has also been identified as the sister of Martha and Lazarus (see Luke 10:38-42; John 11). The Eastern Catholic and Orthodox Churches, on the other hand, have always seen this Mary as a different woman.

There is no doubt that initially Mary was a woman in need of a deliverer. And it is clear that the woman who encountered the risen Christ at the empty tomb was the one and only Mary Magdalene (see Matthew 28:1-10; Mark 16:9; John 20:11-18). Mary's life, as measured in Scripture passages, moves from that initial encounter with Jesus to her position as the first eyewitness and evangelist of his resurrection.

John's Gospel describes Mary arriving at Jesus' tomb by herself. She saw that the stone—which blocked the entrance to the tomb—had been removed. She also saw that the tomb was empty. But in relaying the news to the apostles, she didn't say that Jesus had risen—at least not yet. Instead she said, "They have taken the Lord from the tomb, and we don't know where they put him" (John 20:2).

Then Peter and the "disciple whom Jesus loved"—Tradition identifies him as the apostle John—raced to the tomb (John 20:2). Peter saw the empty tomb but didn't understand that Jesus had risen from the dead. The other disciple believed, though Scripture doesn't indicate that he shared his thoughts with anyone (see John 20:8).

Both disciples returned home, while Mary remained at the tomb. As she leaned into the entrance and wept, she saw two angels. They asked her, "Woman, why are you weeping?" And she replied, "They have taken my Lord, and I don't know where they laid him" (John 20:13).

Mary then turned away from the tomb. She was surprised to see a man standing there. Thinking he was the gardener, she asked him to tell her where Jesus was, so she could give him a proper burial. Then, Scripture recounts, "Jesus said to her, 'Mary!' She turned and said to him in Hebrew, 'Rabbouni,' which means Teacher" (John 20:16).

The scene goes on to further reveal the depth and richness of the relationship between Jesus and Mary:

> Jesus said to her, "Stop holding on to me, for I have not yet ascended to the Father. But go to my brothers and tell them, 'I am going to my Father and your Father, to my God and your God.'" (John 20:17)

The Greek here describes Mary as *clinging* to Jesus. She could not let go of the One who delivered her from so much evil and, in doing so, changed her life forever. She wanted to be near him, protected and secure in his love. Jesus revealed, however, that he must ascend to his Father. By his ascension, Jesus would complete the paschal mystery and open the way to heaven.

Jesus gave Mary a final bit of instruction: "But go to my brothers and tell them, 'I am going to my Father and your Father, to my God and your God'" (John 20:17). Mary returned to the apostles, exclaiming that she had "seen the Lord" (18) and then telling them everything he said to her.

By sending Mary to share the good news of his resurrection with the apostles, Jesus gave her a new and apostolic role. During the Jubilee Year of Mercy in 2016, Pope Francis acknowledged this by elevating the liturgical celebration of Mary Magdalene to that of a feast day, with the intent that she be venerated in the same manner as the rest of the apostles.

It is truly amazing how God transformed Mary Magdalene's life. She went from being somewhat of an outcast who was spiritually oppressed to being the first apostle of the good news. Mary's life was truly unique, but her story can encourage each of us as we acknowledge that we are in need of spiritual transformation.

That transformation can happen in different ways—for example, through confession, prayer, spiritual accompaniment, or healing. But for every disciple on the highway of life, transformation is an ongoing part of the journey. When we are transformed and cling to Jesus, he becomes our everything. He takes away our fears as he draws us to himself, so that we in turn can share the good news with others as Mary did.

A Modern Transformation

Tom was a shy, well-mannered, sensitive child who rarely spoke up. He blended into the background, so to speak. He was the kind of student teachers love to have in their class.

Tom's parents divorced around the time he left for college. His mother was heartbroken and, for a long time, inconsolable. The entire experience was difficult for Tom as well. It drove a wedge between him and his mother. Hurt feelings, misunderstandings, and arguments became the norm.

After college, Tom married, and the couple had a baby girl. Though Tom was Catholic, baptizing his baby was the last thing on his mind. He didn't have anything against Baptism or the Church, per se. His lack of enthusiasm had more to do with the minor role faith played in his life at the time.

Then Tom happened to meet a priest who helped him see how much God loved him and how Jesus was present to him in every moment of his life. Tom began to experience the transformation that comes with accepting that truth. He became a wholehearted disciple of Jesus Christ and also took up his identity as a Catholic father.

The change wasn't magic, of course; it took time. But through the priest's love and respect for Tom and his family, Tom began going to confession on a regular basis—something he had never done in his life. As his relationship with the priest and God deepened, Tom eventually decided to have his daughter baptized.

Even Tom's home gave evidence of his transformation. He and his wife placed faith-inspiring artwork and sacramentals such as crucifixes on the walls. The Bible and other spiritual books found their way onto tables and bookshelves, and soon their spines were bent and the pages well turned.

Tom and his wife went on to have four more children, each of whom was baptized. Despite their growing family, Tom and his wife felt called by God to be more involved in their parish. Soon they were helping out at men's and women's retreats and serving the homeless.

I've known Tom for most of his life, and I often look to him for spiritual advice. How he and his wife have raised their family—the kind of people they have become—is the stuff of books detailing the lives of the saints. I often tell people in my parish that I am privileged to have so many photos that capture Tom and me together, because one day he will be a saint, and those pictures will become holy cards! Tom has been a tremendous example of the kind of spiritual transformation that can happen when we let God love us.

FOR REFLECTION

1. How does Mary Magdalene's story challenge or inspire you? Do you think you need spiritual transformation? Name one small way you can come closer to God's will for your life.

2. Are there areas in your life that need healing? Or do you need to be reconciled with someone who has hurt you or whom you have hurt? Consider how the Sacrament of Reconciliation can help you find forgiveness

and the courage to move forward, and then take advantage of this healing gift of God to the Church.

3. How have you encountered Jesus in your life? If you feel you haven't, or if the experience is a distant memory, ask God to step in now to renew you and bring you to deeper transformation through his personal love for you.

FOR PRAYER

Lord, you call us to be like you. But for this to happen, we must allow you to transform our lives—including the things that we value and the choices we make. Help us be more open to your grace and to recognize that with you, change leads to blessing—not only for ourselves but for others. Amen.

CHAPTER 3

St. Lawrence, Deacon

Seeing Christ as Someone
Worth Dying For

Although this chapter highlights the martyrdom of St. Law-rence, a third-century archdeacon—or chief deacon—of Rome, I would like to honor all those who have given their lives for Jesus Christ. Martyrs (witnesses) are a testament to radical faith, love, and sacrifice in every age. The liturgical calendar attests to the incredible number of martyrs throughout the centuries and across cultures.

For example, the seven men and five women known as the Scillitan martyrs (AD 180) were the first documented African martyrs. They were from the town of Scillium, in present-day Tunisia. They were taken to Carthage, where they were interrogated for refusing to worship the Roman emperor. Unlike most Christian martyrs of their time, they were offered thirty days to recant. Upon their refusal, they were put to death by the sword. Their feast day is July 17.

Only a few decades later, in AD 203, Sts. Perpetua and Felicity and several companions were martyred in Carthage. Perpetua, who was of noble lineage, had a Christian mother and a pagan father. The authorities arrested her for publicly proclaiming her Christian faith.

While in prison, Perpetua met Felicity, a pregnant slave, who had also been condemned for proclaiming her faith in Christ. Felicity delivered her baby while in prison and gave the baby to a free Christian to raise. The feast day for these North African martyrs is March 7.

In the nineteenth century, a great persecution of Christians broke out in Korea, where missionaries from China and elsewhere proclaimed the good news of Jesus Christ. Among those martyred were Sts. Andrew Kim (1821–1846) and Paul Chong Hasang (1795–1839). Andrew Kim, the first Korean-born Catholic priest, was twenty-five when he was tortured and killed for his efforts to spread the Catholic faith. Paul Chong Hasang was a lay missionary who channeled his diplomatic abilities into setting up the first Catholic vicariate, or territorial jurisdiction, in Korea. He also convinced the bishop of Beijing to send more missionaries to Korea.

In 1984 Pope John Paul II canonized Andrew Kim and Paul Chong Hasang, along with 102 additional Korean martyrs. Their feast day is September 20.

Patron of Deacons

I'm a deacon, and like most deacons, I love St. Lawrence. Call it favoritism if you must, but I had to feature him. Lawrence is the patron saint of deacons, chefs, and firefighters. Why this is so will make more sense after you read his story.

Lawrence was born in Spain in the first half of the third century. Dioceses were fairly new then. Deacons tended to operate regionally and at the request of the local bishop. As a deacon, Lawrence was responsible for helping the bishop meet the physical and spiritual needs of his community. This ministry of charity finds its roots in the New Testament:

> At that time, as the number of disciples continued to grow, the Hellenists complained against the Hebrews because their widows were being neglected in the daily distribution. So the Twelve called together the community of the disciples and said, "It is not right for us to neglect the word of God to serve at table. Brothers, select from among you seven reputable men, filled with the Spirit and wisdom, whom we shall appoint to this task, whereas we shall devote ourselves to prayer and to the ministry of the word." (Acts 6:1-4)

The word "deacon," from the Greek *diakonos,* literally means "servant" or "server." It's not referring to someone who waits on tables, as some might think based on this biblical passage; the diaconal ministry is broader than that. It includes serving at the table of the Lord—the altar—by assisting priests at the liturgy, but it also involves doing whatever the bishop or parish priest needs them to do. That might be teaching; baptizing; presiding at funeral services; organizing a soup kitchen; serving the poor, the needy, the sick, those isolated at home or in institutions; and so on.

The passage from the Acts of the Apostles addresses the need for leaders who would advocate, in an official capacity, on behalf of the Hellenist Jews—that is, the Greek-influenced Jews—so they could receive their fair share of food and alms. The Hebrew Jews, in these very early days after the resurrection of Jesus, tended to look down on the Hellenist Jews, because many of the Hellenists mixed Jewish tradition with elements from Greek culture. Marginalized by their more "orthodox" Hebrew counterparts, the Hellenist disciples needed advocates, and these would be the deacons.

Following this tradition of the deacon as servant-advocate, Lawrence eventually found himself responsible for all the church's charitable activities in the Diocese of Rome. Pope Sixtus II put him in charge of making sure that all widows, orphans, sick, and poor persons received what they needed. Not long after receiving his new appointment, Lawrence, along with Pope Sixtus and several other deacons, fell victim to the Emperor Valerian's edict condemning Christianity. They were arrested, and Pope Sixtus was put to death on August 6, 258.

The emperor offered to spare Lawrence's life in exchange for all the wealth in the diocesan treasuries. Tradition has it that the emperor gave Lawrence time to go and collect the money. Instead Lawrence emptied the treasuries and gave the money to the poor, after which he returned to the emperor to present the treasure he *had* collected—not silver and gold but the poor, the sick, and the widowed. These, he advised as he presented them to the emperor, were the true riches of the Church.

Lawrence's love for Christ and his passionate advocacy for the poor led to his death. According to tradition, he was burned to death on a gridiron, saying at one point, "Turn me over. I'm done on this side!" Thus his patronage of chefs and firefighters—and perhaps humorists.

Lawrence's witness of faith has left a lasting impression not only on deacons but on the entire Church. His feast day is August 10.

Love Is at the Heart of Martyrdom

The word "martyr" comes from the Latin *martyrium,* which literally means "witness." In a Christian context, martyrs witness to their faith in the most extreme way by sacrificing their lives for the sake of Jesus Christ. Jesus speaks of this radical form of self-sacrifice in the Gospel of Matthew: "Whoever wishes to come after me must deny himself, take up his cross, and follow me. For whoever wishes to save his life will lose it, but whoever loses his life for my sake will find it" (Matthew 16:24-25).

Taking up your cross and embracing your death for the sake of the kingdom is essential for discipleship. But not everyone is called to literally die for their faith. For most of us, the stakes aren't that high. Jesus admits as much when he speaks of persecutions that disciples will have to endure—for example, slander and lies—for the sake of his name (see Matthew 5:11-12; John 15:20).

While not on a par with sacrificing one's life, bearing the slings and arrows of others because of your beliefs can be daunting. It can in fact require no small amount of heroism. Dying to self comes in all shapes and sizes, ranging from dealing with an unkind word or a verbal assault on your character to "laying down your life for a friend" (John 15:13).

In other words, we see our sacrificial witness to the faith in a broad context, highlighting all the things, great and small, that we do (or do not do) in the face of persecution. These are the ways in which we heed the words of Jesus to pray for our persecutors and to love our enemies (see Matthew 5:44). When you get down to it, martyrdom is all about how we choose to love those who don't love us in return.

A priest-friend of mine, we will call him Fr. Tom, has witnessed to his faith through an experience that nearly cost him his life. His was a late vocation, coming after his young adult life as a high school teacher. (Fr. Tom was a huge Elvis fan. He had been to Graceland so often that he could have given the tour himself.)

Before he began to consider the priesthood, Tom had wanted to be a dad. His extended family included a number of adopted nieces and nephews, so Tom started thinking about adoption. After completing all the screening and paperwork, he adopted an eight-year-old boy.

As with all adoptions, it was a loving gesture but not without its challenges. Tom's son came from a broken home and had already spent time in foster settings that had left their mark in the form of psychological and behavioral issues. These issues would play out in dramatic and violent fashion.

During an argument, his son, who was seventeen by that time, pulled a sawed-off shotgun from underneath his coat and shot Tom in the stomach at point-blank range. Tom was rushed to the hospital, where the emergency room doctors were able to remove the slug from his abdomen.

Tom's son was charged with assault with intent to commit murder, and he spent fifteen years in prison. At his sentencing, the son asked his father for forgiveness, and Tom honored his request. For the next several years, Tom visited his son in prison.

Reflecting on this time in his life, Fr. Tom told me that he believes strongly that God kept him alive for a reason. He discovered that reason later, in the priesthood. He won't acknowledge it, because he is humble, but Fr. Tom has spent his life as a priest sharing God's mercy and changing lives for the better.

Fr. Tom's willingness to return love for hate makes him a worthy example of what it means to lay down your life for someone. It is also why he chose a vocation that would position him to help others do the same.

FOR REFLECTION

1. Was there a particular aspect of St. Lawrence's story you found compelling? Why? Consider asking Lawrence to pray that you have the courage to witness to your faith in whatever way you are called to witness.

2. Thinking of a martyr as a "witness," who has been an inspiring martyr of the faith in your life?

3. Martyrdom comes down to how we choose to love those who do not love us in return. How has God called you to do this?

FOR PRAYER

Lord, you call your disciples to take up their cross and follow you. Help us be mindful of the fact that each of us has a different cross to bear. Give us the courage, in the face of persecution, to return a blessing for a curse and to respond to hatred with love. Amen.

CHAPTER 4

St. Augustine

Seeing God in Our Deepest Desires

Our desires are gifts from God. Even our baser desires hide within them a kernel of truth. And truth—wherever it is found—points us to Jesus, who is "the way and the truth and the life" (John 14:6).

In his novel *The World, the Flesh and Father Smith,* the mid-twentieth-century Scottish writer Bruce Marshall presents a clever debate between the story's protagonist, Fr. Smith, and a woman who is convinced that religion is merely a substitute for sex. During the course of the debate, Fr. Smith remarks, "The young man who rings the bell at the brothel is unconsciously looking for God."[2]

This quote—often mistakenly attributed to G. K. Chesterton—highlights the fundamental though often unconscious orientation of the human heart toward God. While at times we might pursue desires that lead us away from God, underneath them is a longing for the infinite that only God can satisfy.

St. Augustine was certainly a man of desires. Among other things, he had a desire for respect, love, and knowledge. He pursued each of these desires with dogged determination, and the further he pursued, the closer he came to Christ. Through his autobiography, *Confessions*, Augustine invites us into the world of his desires and his many attempts to satisfy them. Following these desires would eventually lead Augustine to pen one of the most famous lines in all of Christian theology: "You have made us for yourself, and our heart is restless until it rests in you."[3]

The Desire for Respect

Augustine was born in AD 354 in Thagaste, in present-day Algeria. In his book *Augustine of Hippo*, famed biographer Peter Brown suggests that from an early age, Augustine wanted to make a name for himself, to be respected. In the municipality of Thagaste, dominated as it was by agrarian life, one sure way "off the farm" was through education. Like his intellectual hero, Cicero, whose *Hortensius* first ignited Augustine's love of rhetoric and philosophy, Augustine wanted to be a famous *rhetor*—a public speaker and teacher of rhetoric. He dreamt of speaking on behalf of an influential enterprise or philosophical society, or even for the Roman Empire through a position in the imperial court.

Augustine's parents, Patricius and Monica (that's St. Monica), recognized their son's ambition and abilities early on and were united in their attempts to offer him the best opportunities for success. Unfortunately, as a poor farmer, Patricius was unable to fund Augustine's dreams himself, but he had powerful friends. He benefitted from the patronage of an influential citizen of Thagaste named Romanianus, who was wealthy and also well-connected in Rome.

Men like Romanianus financially backed prospects, such as budding scholars and athletes, whose eventual success would increase their patron's influence and prestige. Through the patronage of Romanianus and others, Augustine won the opportunity to pursue higher studies in Carthage and later in Rome and Milan. Augustine's talents as a teacher, speaker, and philosopher were obvious and soon well-known.

Shortly after his arrival in Rome, Augustine received an enviable post as a professor of rhetoric in Milan. It is there that he encountered the local bishop, St. Ambrose, a formidable *rhetor*, philosopher, and theologian. Ambrose offered Augustine a different kind of patronage—not one that led to further wealth and the secular respect that comes with it but one that led to Christian Baptism and later, as a successor to the apostles, to being one of the most famous theologians in Christian history.

After his conversion, Augustine would write prolifically, challenging such heresies of his day as Manicheism and Docetism. Yet he wanted to pursue a monastic life like that of his mentor, Ambrose. He returned to North Africa to found his own religious community. As sometimes happens, however, God had other plans.

Augustine's work was becoming known throughout the Roman Empire, particularly his writing that brought together Greek philosophy and the teachings of Scripture. His reputation preceded his return to Africa. Because of his fame and ability, the church in Hippo conscripted him into the priesthood in the year 391. Four years later, by popular acclaim of the people, he was consecrated bishop of Hippo.

From his *cathedra* or "bishop's chair," Augustine's desire for respect took on a new focus. His work and his achievements were no longer about garnering greater personal success and notoriety. His heart was now completely oriented toward Christ. He wanted the world to respect and love Christ and his Church. As a preacher, pastor of souls, and writer, Augustine became a *rhetor* for Christ and for the kingdom of God.

The Desire for Love

Augustine's *Confessions* reveal that, as a young man, he struggled with lust—a struggle captured in his plea to the Lord: "Grant me chastity and continence, but not yet."[4] These words reveal his understanding that chastity is a gift from God. It was a gift God had been trying to give but that Augustine hadn't been ready or willing to accept.

Augustine's struggles with chastity notwithstanding, he also had a deep desire for committed love with a woman and for the filial love that occurs between parent and child. For fifteen years he had a monogamous relationship with a concubine, and they had a son, Adeodatus ("given by God").

In book eight of his *Confessions,* Augustine describes his moment of conversion. At home with his friend Alypius, Augustine was in turmoil as he struggled with the question of embracing Christianity and its moral imperatives. He went into the garden and threw himself down under a fig tree, in tears and an agony of indecision. Suddenly he heard a child in a nearby house chanting, "Pick up and read, pick up and read."

The Epistles of St. Paul were at hand, and opening the book at random, Augustine's eyes fell on a passage that dispelled all doubt: "Not in riots and drunken parties, not in eroticism and indecencies, not in strife and revelry, but put on the Lord Jesus Christ and make no provision for the flesh in its lusts" (see Romans 13:13-14).[5]

After his conversion, Augustine and his concubine parted, but Adeodatus remained with Augustine, and together they were baptized by Ambrose. (Monica died shortly after Augustine's and Adeodatus' Baptisms, having seen her constant prayers for her son's conversion finally bear fruit. Sadly, a year later, Adeodatus also died.)

Augustine's *Confessions* reveal his deep love for his concubine, whose name he never discloses. Unfortunately, concubinage was the only path available to them. Romans understood marriage to be a contractual agreement predicated on the accumulation of wealth. Men and women of different socioeconomic classes were forbidden to marry. In light of this, Augustine's mother, Monica, had insisted that he leave the woman and marry someone of his own class. She even tried to arrange a marriage for him, an effort that grieved Augustine terribly. Eventually he sent the unnamed woman away, and he never married.

Augustine found his deepest love *after* his conversion. In one of the most beautiful lines in his *Confessions*, Augustine writes intimately of God's pursuit of him and how slow he was to respond to that love: "Late have I loved you, beauty so old and so new: late have I loved you."[6]

After his conversion, Augustine claimed Christ as the fulfillment of his deepest desire for love. This in turn led him to embrace a celibate life as a priest and bishop, by which— through his preaching and writing—he shared his love for Christ with his congregation and eventually the world.

The Desire for Knowledge

Early in his life, Augustine seemed to want knowledge primarily because it would garner respect for his abilities. Knowledge was Augustine's way out of Thagaste and into the big city, where he could work as a *rhetor*. While studying in Carthage, Augustine's desire for knowledge deepened. He began to appreciate the nobility and power of truth for its own sake. Consequently he became a philosopher, a term derived from the Greek *philosophos*, meaning "lover of wisdom."

At Carthage Augustine became involved with the Manicheans, the philosophical sect founded by Mani. Mani was a self-proclaimed prophet who taught a dualist view of the cosmos, in which the universe was divided into good and evil. Mani and his followers considered all matter to be evil; they only considered the spiritual to be good. This view clashed with Judeo-Christian teaching, which views the universe as created by God and therefore good.

Manichean cosmology initially persuaded Augustine. Its tenets about the evilness of matter seemed to be proved by his own struggles with the weakness of the flesh. Through the teaching of Ambrose, however, Augustine gradually adopted a Christian worldview, becoming convinced of the truth of Christ, his love, and his lordship over the universe. He saw that God was good, which meant that his creation was also good. Moreover, God doesn't create evil things. Evil, Augustine would later write, is a privation of the good, an absence of it.

After his Baptism, Augustine turned his mind and heart toward Christ, whom he now saw as the source of all knowledge and truth. As bishop of Hippo, he would be devoted to reflecting on and sharing this truth.

Thus Augustine set aside his desires for respect, love, and knowledge and embraced a life of discipleship. This was not an exchange of one set of desires for another. Rather his Christianity marked a deepening and fulfillment of his desires.

From Atheist to Theology Teacher

I spent five years as an adult faith formation director in the Archdiocese of Washington, DC. During that time, I had the pleasure of directing the Rite of Christian Initiation of Adults (RCIA), now referred to as the Order of Christian Initiation of Adults (OCIA). One year I had a particularly large class—twenty-five people from all walks of life—including a snarky self-professed atheist we'll call Herman.

On the first day of RCIA, Herman told me, "You're going to have a hard time convincing me of this stuff." To which I responded, "I don't have to convince you. God will do that for me. Just keep coming to our meetings."

Herman was a confident man who had the world on a string. A graduate of an Ivy League school, he enjoyed a lucrative position as an attorney who represented some very exclusive clients. Herman was also outspoken, never slow to question or to speak his mind. At first this created some tension in the group. Herman was a force to be reckoned with.

But as others were coming to believe in the Catholic faith, Herman found himself having to engage not only me but many others in debates about the truth of Christianity. Persuasive arguments from Scripture and Church teaching, along with the witness of the saints—a potent combination indeed—continually challenged his atheistic principles. Added to this was the witness of faith percolating among the other catechumens and candidates. Herman began to wear down.

Over time, Herman stopped trying to defend his atheism and began to study the faith on its own terms and for its own sake. I began to see Herman at Mass and at parish events. I heard reports that he and his family were helping at a local homeless shelter and praying outside Planned Parenthood.

By the time Lent rolled around, it was obvious that Herman was completely invested in his formation. He studied endlessly, channeling his desire for truth into study of the Scriptures. At one point, Herman asked me for a suggested reading list and the names of podcasts he could listen to that would further his study. I was completely amazed by his transformation and his commitment.

Halfway through Lent, Herman asked to meet with me outside of our weekly sessions. Over coffee, he confessed that, although he did like the idea of receiving Communion with his wife and children, who were already Catholic, his original intention in joining RCIA was to pacify his wife and to prove to himself that Catholicism was at worst a sham and at best a security blanket. But things began to change. He found himself compelled to read Scripture and to study the *Catechism*. He wanted to be at Mass for himself and not just in support of his family.

When I asked Herman what caused the change, he said, "It has to be God, because at the beginning of RCIA, I didn't imagine myself being Catholic, nor did I want to be." He went on to say, "Now, being Catholic is all I want." When I asked Herman why he wanted to be Catholic, he said that he had come to believe in Jesus Christ and that the Church was his home. If he wanted to be with Christ, he needed to be in the Church.

Herman was baptized that Easter. After a few years passed, I received a surprise message from him on Facebook. He had moved his family from Washington, DC, to a small town in Missouri, and he had left the legal profession to become a high school theology teacher! He said that he never saw this coming, and he was the happiest he had ever been. Herman had found God in his deepest desires.

FOR REFLECTION

1. Reflect on your desires over the years. Which of these have been fulfilled? Which have not? As far as you are able to determine, do you know why your desires have been fulfilled or why they haven't?

2. Our desire for God grows when we see how he has led us through life and when we are mindful of his blessings. How has God led you? In what specific ways do you think he's involved in your life right now?

3. What is it about Jesus that compels you to desire eternity with him? Identify some books, websites, podcasts, or other media that can help you grow in your knowledge of and desire for him.

FOR PRAYER

Lord, I don't always desire you as I should. My heart often chases after interests and goals that ultimately fail to satisfy. Help me desire you the way you desire me: with unfailing love and commitment. Amen.

CHAPTER 5

St. Francis of Assisi

Seeing Creation as
Our Common Home

Most of us have a place to call home, but many people do not. This harsh reality eclipses the truth that God intended his creation as a home for all, where everyone could "be fruitful and multiply" (Genesis 1:28, RSVCE). When our own interests and pursuit of comfort supersede charity and solidarity, the world becomes a little less human and a little less of a home to anyone.

Throughout the centuries, saints like Benedict of Nursia (480–547), Kateri Tekakwitha (1656–1680), and Pope Paul VI (1897–1978) have reminded us, in their own unique ways, that creation is our common home and that everyone belongs. And probably no one lived this truth better than St. Francis of Assisi.

Francis didn't always see the world this way. God had to intervene in his life through a series of difficult circumstances before Francis could see this truth. He would lose all he had, even his own home, before recognizing the home that God had given him. It was a home complete with family members: the trees, the sky, the sun, the flowers, the animals, and the marginalized of society.

Youthful Dreams

Born in the late twelfth century in Assisi, Italy, Francis was the son of an affluent textile merchant. He lived a life of luxury and relative ease, and his wealth provided opportunities that most people could only dream of. Early on, Francis had many dreams for his future. He dreamed of being a nobleman. He also dreamed of being a soldier and an adventurer.

The practicalities of life pushed such dreams aside, as they so often do. Francis resigned himself to adopting the family trade. Such was the social expectation for every child of Assisi, but for Francis it was a rude awakening. He became a cloth merchant, like his father.

Francis set out to follow the family plan, working as an apprentice to his father. But God began to intervene in his life during his young adult years, under the guise of dramatic circumstances. These circumstances would place Francis in a position of dependency on a level he hadn't known.

Civil war broke out between Assisi and the Papal States. Francis joined the resistance and fought to protect the autonomy of his beloved city. Eventually he was captured and imprisoned in the neighboring town of Perugia. After the war, his father ransomed him, and Francis returned home. But he was terribly ill from his confinement.

After a long convalescence, Francis once again pursued his desire for adventure, fame, and fortune. Much to his parents' surprise, he joined a battalion on crusade to the Holy Land. On the way, however, Francis had a peculiar dream, in which heard a voice:

> "Francis, who can do better for thee, the lord or the servant, the rich man or the poor?" And when Francis had made reply that alike the lord and the rich man could do the best, the Voice answered forthwith, "Why, then, dost thou leave the Lord for the servant, the rich God for a poor mortal?" And Francis said, "Lord, what wilt Thou have me to do?" And the Lord said unto him, "Return unto thy country, for the vision that thou hast seen betokeneth that which shall be spiritually wrought, and is to be fulfilled in thee not by mortal counsel, but by divine."[7]

Upon waking, Francis headed home to seek God's will. On the outskirts of Assisi, he encountered a leper. He had an intense fear of leprosy, and rightly so. At that time, no one knew how the disease spread. Conventional wisdom suggested that the only safe response was to avoid leprous persons altogether. Lepers were condemned to live in colonies, far from any towns and villages and their own homes and loved ones. They would pace the roadsides begging for alms, careful not to get too close to passersby. They were like the living dead.

Francis saw the leprous man with new eyes. Perhaps his experience of being incarcerated or his long convalescence prompted him to get off his horse and approach the man. Francis gave him some money, which was customary, but he felt compelled to do more. Moved by compassion, Francis kissed the leper's hands, then walked back to his horse. Turning around to look at the decrepit figure one more time, Francis was shocked to find that he had vanished. Francis knew in his heart that he had encountered Jesus Christ.

As he pondered what this event meant for him, Francis committed himself to prayer and almsgiving. With every coin and piece of clothing he gave away, he began to feel greater joy and peace. He was close to finding his purpose. There was something exciting and freeing about the idea of depending entirely on God—an idea that would soon become a reality.

Dissatisfied with the trappings of conventional life, Francis began to feel more at home in the wilderness surrounding Assisi. The environment suited his desire for simplicity and austerity. He spent hours in seclusion, praying and meditating, trying to discern what God might want from him.

One night, while in the nearby chapel of San Damiano, Francis heard a voice speak to him three times from the crucifix, urging him to "go and repair my church, which as you can see is in ruins."[8] Francis discerned this to be the voice of God—a second encounter. Being somewhat pragmatic, he examined his surroundings and decided that God was speaking of the chapel, which had been abandoned for some time and had fallen into disrepair. To pay for the restoration,

Francis sold not only his own possessions but also cloth from his father's inventory.

God's plan for Francis soon became public, and in dramatic fashion. Furious that his son had been selling his textiles without his permission and putting the proceeds toward rebuilding the derelict chapel, Francis' father demanded justice. At the bishop's court, with many townspeople looking on—gossip travels quickly in small towns—Francis' father pleaded his case. Having heard from Francis also, the bishop decided that the young man should repay his father in full.

Francis' recent encounters with God assured him that everything was happening according to God's design—even the humiliation he was experiencing, even the bishop's unsympathetic verdict. In that moment, Francis adopted the radicalism that was to become the hallmark of his life. Happy to make a public spectacle of himself if it meant doing God's will, he removed all of his clothes and handed them over to his father, as if to say, *These too are yours. Take them as part of my repayment.* With this stunning gesture, Francis publicly renounced his claim to his father's inheritance.

A New Adventure

To survive Francis would have to trust in divine providence. There was no other way. His life began to revolve around prayer, preaching, and begging for necessities. Christ became the reason for his being, and the gospel his blueprint for living. He began to see many things differently. There was no longer a difference between a leprous person and a healthy person, a rich person and a poor person: every human being—regardless of wealth or status—was a child of God.

As for adventure, Francis put away his dreams of military heroism. Now no adventure would be greater than that of helping others respond to Christ in faith.

Living among the gifts of creation, Francis felt closer to the Giver of those gifts than he ever had before. Everything was God's, which in a sense made every human being a beggar like himself. Most were blind to their poverty—their poverty of spirit—which is why so many people, like his father, spent their lives climbing social ladders and accumulating wealth and material possessions, things that were thought to be the marks of success and dignity.

Francis found himself at home in nature. It was the house that God had provided for all his children. Everything in this house belonged to God. Everyone, even the leper, had a place in this common home.

Rumors spread throughout Assisi that Francis talked to the animals and the elements as if they were his family members, that he gave homilies to the birds, and even that he tamed a wild wolf through the Sign of the Cross and a few kind words. Time and again people from surrounding towns and villages left their civilized lives behind for a while to go and see Francis in his environment—this common home where all were welcome.

The motivations of these inquirers varied. Some came thinking they'd see a freak who had lost his mind. Others came purely out of concern for Francis. Still others came to discover the power that was animating him—a man who didn't have a coin to his name yet seemed to wear the smile of a man who had everything.

Some people stayed for a while and listened to Francis preach. Some helped with renovations to the chapel. Still others discovered that their home was with Francis, the creation he had befriended, and the God he encountered there.

Francis spent the rest of his life witnessing to the truth of God's love for humanity. He did this primarily through preaching and calling people to repentance. His life was an example of radical dependence on God as well as on the stewardship of creation.

Francis eventually founded a new religious order, the Order of Friars Minor, whose members today are commonly referred to as Franciscans. The Franciscan Order is a *mendicant* order—an order of beggars who give themselves to the service of others, especially those at the bottom of the social ladder. Franciscans have played a significant role in the renewal of the Catholic Church through the centuries, and they still have a profound impact today. Their power and influence stem in part from their conviction that we are all brothers and sisters. We are all part of one family—the family of God—and we all share a common home, God's creation.

Each of us needs to see the world as St. Francis did. The question is, will we allow God to intervene and change the course of our lives, perhaps radically, in order to see this way? If doing so means living life to the full (see John 10:10), then sign me up!

Adopting the Franciscan Way

Pope Francis' values are similar to those of St. Francis, as is evident in the simple fact that he chose his papal name in honor of the saint from Assisi. This Jesuit pope and follower of St. Ignatius has founded his papacy on the twin pillars of the Franciscan way of life: first, charity and service toward others, particularly the poor and most vulnerable; and second, the stewardship of God's creation.

Even before he was Pope Francis, Jorge Bergolio embraced a life of simplicity and austerity. As the archbishop of Buenos Aires, he spent much of his time walking the streets of the barrios, listening to the cries of the poor, celebrating Mass with them, alleviating their suffering when he could, and offering them comfort and hope. He generally traveled around the city by bus, refusing the car available to him.

In Rome prior to the conclave, Francis avoided the luxuries available to him. He refused the use of Vatican cars in favor of taxis and walking. After being elected pope, he returned to the hotel where he had stayed prior to the election to pay his bill. Rather than live in the papal palace, he chose to live in the Domus Sanctae Marthae, a simple, plainly furnished guest house for clergy. As bishop of Rome, Francis has put the marginalized first, favoring, for example, to build a homeless shelter rather than renovate an ancient church.

For his first papal visit, Francis chose to go to the obscure island of Lampedusa in the Mediterranean Sea, midway between the coasts of southern Italy and northern Libya. He made this trip against the advice of his secretary of state, who thought he should visit a larger, well-known country. But Lampedusa is a stopping point for many undocumented migrants on their way to Europe, a perilous journey on crowded and poorly equipped boats. Such trips can end in the tragedy of migrants drowning when their boats go down. Migrants who do reach shore face the ever-present danger of human trafficking that haunts migration routes.

Using a chalice made from the wreckage of migrant ships, Pope Francis offered Mass in Lampedusa. There he preached about the need for humanity to recover its sense of solidarity, a sense that he would later link to the universal need to see creation as our common home. Francis took up this theme in his encyclical letter *Laudato Si*. This encyclical reminds us that, from the beginning, creation has been the home that God gave humanity. And like any home, creation must be cared for by those who live in it.

The world is indeed a place filled with energy, life, and possibility, but it's also limited. Therefore Christians should look upon the care of creation as more than environmental consciousness. It is a critical aspect of Christian morality, implicit in Jesus' command to love one's neighbor as oneself (see Mark 12:31).

FOR REFLECTION

1. Does the life of St. Francis inspire or challenge you in any way? Consider how you might allow God to speak to you through the examples of personal surrender to God's will that mark St. Francis' life.

2. Where or when do you feel *at home*? Who or what makes you feel this way? In what ways can you acknowledge and thank those who create a sense of home for you? How can you create that sense of home for others?

3. Do you take the time to be grateful for the gift of creation? If not, why not? How can you express that gratitude in the way you live your daily life and how you use the resources of the earth?

FOR PRAYER

Lord, help me see creation as the home for all humanity. When I am tempted to be wasteful, help me be prudent. When I am tempted toward selfishness, help me be generous. When I am tempted to judge others, help me be humble.

May I always remember, Lord, that creation belongs to you. I am only its steward. Amen.

CHAPTER 6

St. Thomas Aquinas

Seeing the Reasonableness of Faith

The Western Church today is struggling to evangelize as it faces the ongoing secularization of culture—with its consumerism, individualism, religious apathy, and in some quarters, religious intolerance. Materialism, a hallmark of this culture, views the cosmos and everything in it as made up solely of matter. It leaves little room for the spiritual within the created order and certainly no room for the Creator.

According to surveys from the Pew Research Center, over the past ten years there has been an annual increase in Americans who identify as "nones." This category includes people who identify as agnostic or atheist and those who have no religious affiliation in particular. Alongside the social, cultural, and political factors influencing this increase, we must include the trending tendency to view science as the ultimate good.

Many people today view science—particularly the hard sciences, such as physics, chemistry, and biology—as the arbiters of what is real and what is true. Catholics, especially Catholic young people, are not immune to this trend. The Catholic Church, of course, views science as a great good and encourages and participates in scientific exploration and research. But science offers only one avenue toward understanding and explaining our universe.

While science and reason play critical roles in human progress, for the disciple of Christ, they are only part of the picture. Faith is important as well. The Catholic Church teaches that faith and reason are, in fact, complementary:

> "Though faith is above reason, there can never be any real discrepancy between faith and reason. Since the same God who reveals mysteries and infuses faith has bestowed the light of reason on the human mind, God cannot deny himself, nor can truth ever contradict truth." "Consequently, methodical research in all branches of knowledge, provided it is carried out in a truly scientific manner and does not override moral laws, can never conflict with the faith, because the things of the world and the things of faith derive from the same God. The humble and persevering investigator of the secrets of nature is being led, as it were, by the hand of God in spite of himself, for it is God, the conserver of all things, who made them what they are."[9]

We don't have to choose between faith and reason. We need both. No one understood this better than St. Thomas Aquinas. A maverick for his time, Aquinas was not afraid to engage science and reason, because he saw the reason-ability of faith. For God is the source of human reason. But God also transcends human reason, making faith—and therefore theology—necessary for understanding both God and his creation.

Discovering Truth

Born sometime between 1225 and 1227 near the town of Aquino, Italy, Aquinas was on the path to religious life from the time he was five years old. His parents enrolled him in the Benedictine Abbey of Monte Casino, where he completed a classical education before enrolling at the age of fourteen or fifteen at the University of Naples. There he encountered the metaphysics of Aristotle for the first time.

Metaphysics, in Aristotle's day, was the study of the causes and principles of being: how something came to be and why it is what it is and not something else. Metaphysics (literally, "after" or "beyond" physics) also left room for the study of eternal beings, which Aristotle described as *theology*. Throughout Thomas' education, he reflected on and debated the metaphysics of Aristotle, always trying to convince others of the goodness of the created order and the need to apply human reason to divine faith.

Eventually Aquinas joined the Order of Preachers, com-monly referred to as the Dominicans. He completed his education under the tutelage of St. Albert the Great, a renowned scientist and fellow devotee of Aristotle. Aquinas went on to become a prolific writer, a noted theologian, a famed but controversial university professor, and a theological advisor to Popes Alexander IV and Urban IV.

The controversy surrounding Aquinas had to do, in part, with his appreciation for the Muslim philosophers Avicenna and Averroes—two contemporaries who had found uses for Aristotle's metaphysics within Islamic theology. At the time, the Church was still embroiled in the Crusades. Christians looked upon Middle Eastern theology and philosophy with suspicion, even hatred. Aquinas put his own reputation into question and his future in jeopardy simply because he appreciated the teachings of these two Muslim scholars. Aquinas argued that the truth was the truth no matter where it was found. God can use everyone and everything—from the physical laws of the universe, to the flourishing of human relationships, to the challenges of coping with one's perceived enemies—to communicate his truth.

During this period, there was a great deal of theological controversy about the Eucharist. Was it merely a symbol, or was it literally the Real Presence of Jesus Christ under the appearance of bread and wine? Straying too far in the direction of symbol would make the bread and wine used in the celebration of the Mass almost meaningless. Going too far in a literal direction, which many theologians of the time were doing, raised concerns about receiving Communion.

For example, some people said that by chewing the consecrated bread, the faithful were literally chewing the body of the risen and ascended Jesus and therefore causing him harm. This misunderstanding led to stringent Communion practices, such as letting the host dissolve on the tongue instead of chewing it.

Using Aristotle's metaphysics—his categories of matter and form in particular—Aquinas concluded that upon consecration, the essence or *substance* of the bread and wine were changed. Yet their matter, or *accidents*—that is, the properties of bread and wine—remained. Aquinas effectively integrated human reason with divine faith. His proposition, known as *transubstantiation,* later became an official teaching of the Catholic Church.

In his great work, the *Summa Theologica,* Aquinas not only welcomed reason but also used the physical world to explain his understanding of the faith. For example, in his proofs for the existence of God, he used categories like *cause, motion,* and *order* to explain God's existence.

In Aquinas' second proof of the existence of God, he argues that in nature, we observe with our physical senses and deduce with our reason that something cannot cause itself to be. For example, a baby requires conception, and a table does not make itself. The universe, and everything in it, did not cause itself. In order to be, the universe required an *uncaused cause*: that is, a cause that was independent of what it caused and not dependent on anything else in order to be.

In other words, the universe did not cause itself to be. Something outside of it caused it to be, and that something was not dependent on anything else for its existence. Therefore this something is eternal, and this something is God.

Aquinas' *Summa* provides a model for doing theology that inspires Catholic theologians to this day. Because Aquinas was willing to see human reason as a gift from God that can help us understand our faith better, he indicates that faith is reasonable and that theology should always be about faith seeking understanding. Therefore we should not be afraid to engage science and human reason from a faith perspective, and we should welcome truth wherever we find it.

Helping Young People See the Connection between Faith and Reason Today

I've had the privilege of meeting Fr. Robert Spitzer, SJ, a few times. You may have seen this theologian and philosopher's show, *Father Spitzer's Universe,* on EWTN. Or you may have been lucky enough back in 2010 to catch his debate with famed astrophysicist Stephen Hawking on *Larry King Live.*

During our meetings, Fr. Spitzer and I have discussed the declining number of Catholics in the United States, as well as the decreasing enrollment in both Catholic schools and parish religious education programs. While there is no single reason for the decline, he has never failed to cite questions of science in relation to religion as a primary contributor to the difficulty parents, teachers, and catechists have engaging young people in their faith

Fr. Spitzer excels at demonstrating how human reason needs faith in order to grasp the truth, purpose, and meaning of the universe. He does this principally through the work of apologetics. "Apologetics," in a Catholic sense, is the development of reasoned arguments in defense of Church teaching.

After his tenure as the president of Gonzaga University, Fr. Spitzer wanted to develop a science-based approach to apologetics in order to help young Catholics see the reasonableness of their faith in light of scientific discoveries. He understood that for his apologetical approach to be credible, it had to be backed by credible science. So he brought together scientists from all over the country—from such prestigious schools as Harvard, MIT, and the University of Chicago—to help him create teaching materials that would demonstrate how science helps prove the existence of God.

Like Aquinas, Fr. Spitzer chooses to approach teaching about science and faith by engaging scientific theory on its own terms, observing the being of things. This entails, for example, observing the universe's outward expansion from the "Big Bang"—as indicated by background radiation, increasing distances between nearby galaxies, and increasing velocities of heavenly bodies—and deducing from these physical phenomena evidence of the Creator. After all, something had to cause the Big Bang!

Fr. Spitzer's materials use Aquinas' proofs of God's existence to address a variety of scientific hypotheses about how the universe began. For example, one popular hypothesis is that the universe repeatedly expands and contracts, which would imply repeated Big Bangs with every successive expansion. Even in this case, Aquinas' *uncaused cause* proof holds true: something would have to have caused the first of the Big Bangs.

When we pit faith and reason against each other, we end up shortchanging not only ourselves but also God. God wants us to see the reasonableness of our faith, because when we do, we experience not only his transcendence but also his closeness to us. As the psalm says,

All the earth falls in worship before you;
  they sing of you, sing of your name! (Psalm 66:4)

Human reason proposes that creation testifies to God's existence, and our faith confirms that. Faith and reason are complementary gifts from God.

Fr. Spitzer's work can be found at crediblecatholic.com. There you will also see countless testimonies from young people of how his resources have reinspired their faith and changed their lives.

FOR REFLECTION

1. As a person of faith, how willing are you to engage the sciences? If you are not so willing, what is holding you back? Does the fact that the Church welcomes and advances scientific inquiry make a difference in your willingness to engage the sciences going forward?

2. Is there a particular scientific discovery or theory that challenges your faith? Where can you find reliable information to help you grapple with your questions?

3. What have you seen in creation that convinces you there is a Creator? What in creation prevents you from seeing all of creation as a gift from the Creator?

FOR PRAYER

Lord, when you created humanity, you gave us the gift of reason; and throughout the ages, you have invited us to receive the gift of faith. Help me see faith and reason as gifts to use together to glorify you. Help me always strive for a faith that seeks understanding. Amen.

CHAPTER 7

St. Juan Diego

Seeing the Signs
God Gives Us

Whether we know it or not, Catholics are sign watchers. We are formed in the signs of faith, such as sacraments and sacramentals. While we use our physical senses to engage the world around us, we also use our spiritual senses to engage the kingdom of God in our midst. We are formed in the signs of faith.

Jesus calls us to be in the world but not of the world (see John 17:14-19). Our faith keeps us straddling the earthly and the divine. To guide us, God offers us signs that point us toward heaven. These signs range from the natural to the supernatural.

Examples of natural signs: God "makes his sun rise on the bad and the good, and causes rain to fall on the just and the unjust" (Matthew 5:45). And the rainbow is a sign of God's covenant with Noah, pointing to the promise of hope and a renewed creation (see Genesis 9:14-17).

But God also gives us supernatural signs. The sacraments involve the use of natural things—such as water, bread and wine, and oil—for supernatural purposes: salvation, the forgiveness of sin, and commissioning, for example.

There are, of course, any number of ways in which God can give us a sign. But are we looking for these signs? Do we believe that God is trying to speak to us and guide us?

One person who believed God was showing him signs was St. Juan Diego. He received one of the most incredible signs: an apparition of the Blessed Virgin Mary.

Signs from Our Mother

Little is known about the life of Juan Diego Cuauhtlatoatzin (1474–1548). A member of the Chichimeca people in Cuautlitlán, part of modern-day Mexico City, he was married but had no children. When he was fifty years old, Juan and his wife, Maria, were among the first of the Chichimeca to be baptized.

On December 9, 1531, the now-widowed Juan was on his way to Mass when he was visited by the Blessed Virgin Mary, who appeared in a heavenly light. The apparition took place on Tepeyac Hill, on the outskirts of what would become Mexico City. Mary spoke to Juan in his own language of Nahuatl. She told him to speak to the local bishop and convince him to build a shrine to her on Tepeyac Hill, where she would bless all those who invoked her.

It is important to note here that Juan's native name, Cuauht-latoatzin, means "the Talking Eagle" and signifies "one who speaks with great authority." Juan would indeed have to use his authoritative voice to convince the bishop of what he had seen. Initially the bishop didn't believe his story. He asked Juan to give him proof—a sign—that Mary had appeared to him.

Three days later, Juan was looking for a priest to administer the Sacrament of the Anointing of the Sick to his dying uncle when Mary appeared to him again. She told him to gather roses and take them to the bishop as a sign of the truth of Juan's claim. She also told Juan that his uncle would recover.

Even though it was the middle of winter and roses were not in bloom, Juan had no trouble finding and gathering some around Tepeyac. He took the roses to Mary, who arranged them in his *tilma*. When Juan opened this cloak before the bishop and presented the roses to him, an image of Mary was on the interior. The bishop saw this as a convincing sign. When Juan returned home, he found his uncle had fully recovered.

For the rest of his life, Juan lived in a hut next to the church on Tepeyac Hill that the bishop authorized in honor of Mary. Upon Juan's death, he was buried in the church. Pope John Paul II canonized Juan Diego in 2002. His feast day is December 9.

The image of Our Lady of Guadalupe on Juan's *tilma* depicts a young pregnant woman with dark skin and native features. Clothed in a blue mantle dotted with golden stars and standing with the moon under her feet, she is reminiscent of the woman of the Book of Revelation: "a woman clothed with the sun, with the moon under her feet, and on her head a crown of twelve stars" (Revelation 12:1). Like the pregnant Lady of Guadalupe, the woman of Revelation is about to give birth to the Savior (12: 2).

The *tilma* is on display today in the Basilica of Our Lady of Guadalupe in Mexico City. Pope John Paul II declared Our Lady of Guadalupe the patroness of the Americas, and she has become a sign of God's love and care for the Mexican people.

A Garden View

Stacy and I got married in 2007 in a little Catholic church in Oklahoma, which wasn't our home parish. We invited a priest-friend to officiate. Unfortunately, both our wedding rehearsal and the day of the wedding were incredibly stress filled.

Our woes began when members of the wedding party arrived late for the rehearsal. I am a fairly punctual guy, and we were in a high-emotion situation. I tried to look calm as I stared at my watch, nervously waiting for everyone to arrive.

Later, halfway through the rehearsal, the pastor of the parish showed up and began to interrupt and contradict the priest who would officiate at the wedding. The two priests went round and round about things like where the wedding party should sit, whether Stacy and I should sit near each other before the nuptials, and other such logistical points. This was particularly frustrating because the pastor had given permission for our friend to witness our vows. We had no idea that his permission came with a clause that he would try to take over the rehearsal, which ground to a halt.

As the priests took a break, Stacy began to cry. Seeing this, my best man—a friend from South Boston who had a great heart but a fiery temper—approached our priest-friend and said, "You just give the word, Father, and I will knock that other priest out!"

Of course, punching the pastor's lights out was no way to kick off our marriage. So our priest-friend said to Stacy and me, "Look, we'll do things the pastor's way tonight. But tomorrow we'll do things the way we had planned."

The next day, before the ceremony, more problems arose. Family members began airing their dirty laundry (a common occurrence at weddings, for some reason), while guests struggled to find the church. To retreat from all the drama, Stacy and I took a walk through the church gardens.

As we strolled along a path, we noticed how beautiful the trees and bushes were. We heard birds chirping and the babbling of a little stream that ran along the path. All was heavenly! We looked at each other and, at the same time, said, "It's like we're in the Garden of Eden."

We both laughed—something we hadn't done since the beginning of the rehearsal—and we began to reflect on the marriage of Adam and Eve. We thought about how God brought them together and how Adam saw Eve as the *bone of his bones and flesh of his flesh* (see Genesis 2:23). Our reflection helped us remember what our wedding was all about: God and his love for us.

We sat down on a bench next to the stream. Looking at the

water, I was moved by its baptismal significance. I thought about how Jesus used water to demonstrate his love for his disciples in washing their feet. Inspired by this sign, I got down on my knees, took Stacy's shoes off, and began to wash her feet with the water from the stream. Following Jesus' example, I was saying, *I want to serve you, and I delight in doing so.*

I thought about the delight Jesus must have experienced as he washed the feet of his disciples that first night of his passion. He told them that everything that was about to happen was so that "my joy may be in you and your joy may be complete" (John 15:11). I shared my thoughts with Stacy. We laughed and cried. We felt that God was speaking directly to us. His love for us was palpable.

After the wedding ceremony, it started to rain. People were getting soaked as they made for their cars. But as we drove from the church to the reception hall, the rain stopped. As we got out of the car, we noticed that a double rainbow had formed over the reception hall! Again, Stacy and I were filled with the undeniable sense of God's love for us. We looked at each other and said at the same time, "It's like Noah!" As in the Bible, the rainbow was a sign of God's promise of hope and renewal (see Genesis 9:12-17). We knew we were at the start of something wonderful.

The rest of our wedding day was pure bliss. Of course, a lot of factors went into making the day special, but the most important was how Stacy and I looked for God's signs together. We saw these signs as proof that our marriage would be a foretaste of heaven. Those signs have proved true.

FOR REFLECTION

1. If you had been the bishop to whom Juan Diego appealed, would you have needed a sign to convince you of his story? Why do you think the Church carefully weighs claims of Marian apparitions?

2. Have you ever experienced Mary's presence or care in a specific way? How did her care for you deepen your relationship with her?

3. Are you a sign watcher? How do you look for God's signs in your life? What places, events, people, or things have you interpreted as signs of God's love for you? In what ways have those signs led you to be a sign of God's love for others in your daily life?

FOR PRAYER

Happy Juan Diego, true and faithful man! We entrust to you our lay brothers and sisters so that, feeling the call to holiness, they may imbue every area of social life with the spirit of the Gospel. Bless families, strengthen spouses in their marriage, sustain the efforts of parents to give their children a Christian upbringing. Look with favor upon the pain of those who are suffering in body or in spirit, on those afflicted by poverty, loneliness, marginalization or ignorance. May all people, civic leaders and ordinary citizens, always act in accordance with the demands of justice and with respect for the dignity of each person, so that in this way peace may be reinforced.

Beloved Juan Diego, "the talking eagle"! Show us the way that leads to the "Dark Virgin" of Tepeyac, that she may receive us in the depths of her heart, for she is the loving, compassionate Mother who guides us to the true God. Amen.

**—From Pope John Paul II's prayer
at the canonization of St. Juan Diego**[10]

CHAPTER 8

St. Ignatius of Loyola

Seeing God's Will
for Our Lives

W*hat do you want me to do, God?* I can't tell you how
many times I have asked this question. It's a common
one among Catholics and, to be honest, believers in general.
Life is full of crossroads, full of decisions we have to make.

Thankfully, not every decision is of the life-changing or
deal-breaking variety. But there is little dispute that life is
full of moments of discernment. Within the rich heritage
of Catholic spiritualties, one of the greatest discerners ever
was St. Ignatius of Loyola—though, truth be told, St. Francis de Sales gives him a run for his money!

A Spiritual Reset

Born in 1491 near the little town of Azpeitia, Spain, Ignatius spent his early life in and around his family's castle. As a young adult, Ignatius became a courtier and soldier. Courtly life immediately washed over him, nearly drowning him in its drama, intrigue, and sinful delights. His chivalrous disposition frequently gave way to his overpowering desire for pleasure, attention, and spirited competition.

Ignatius was determined to become a military hero. By the age of twenty-six, he had become a knight in the service of one of his noble relatives. But Ignatius' fortunes soon changed. Only four years into his knighthood, at the siege of Pamplona, a cannonball shattered his leg and with it his dreams of honor and prestige.

Unfortunately, the doctors who tended to Ignatius set his leg improperly, and the doctors back in Loyola, where Ignatius went to recover, had to rebreak and reset it. A bone soon began to protrude below the knee, leaving that leg shorter than the other. Unwilling to accept either the notion that he might never realize his dreams of knightly heroism or the thought of walking with a limp, Ignatius persuaded the doctors to cut off the protruding bone and flesh, after which Ignatius would attempt to lengthen his leg through stretching maneuvers. This drastic medical intervention took place without anesthesia, none being available in that era. Ignatius endured great pain and torment—and in the end, he would always walk with a limp.

All this effort shows what kind of man Ignatius was. At his core, he was driven. He had goals, and he was willing to suffer and even die trying to achieve them. In fact, helping others identify their greatest goal, their biggest dream, and judging every decision against it would become the cornerstone of his process of spiritual discernment. But before he could stride along the heights of spirituality, his soul, like his leg, would need to be spiritually reset.

This reset occurred during Ignatius' convalescence. With little to do during his painful recovery, Ignatius asked for reading materials. He was fond of romance novels and tales of knightly chivalry, but the only books available in the family castle were one about the life of Christ and one about the saints. Having no alternative—he wasn't going anywhere—Ignatius read both books many times. Though he had always appreciated and venerated the saints, Ignatius had never wished to imitate them. His heart was still set on the glories of knighthood.

But as Ignatius reflected on his reading, he noted where his thoughts drifted and how he felt emotionally. When he thought about Christ and the saints, he felt a sense of peace and happiness, even excitement. When he considered his former life and his dream of knightly renown, he felt less enthusiastic and ultimately dissatisfied. He began to realize that the saints were showing him a more noble calling and, with it, a deeper honor than knighthood could bestow. A fire began to grow in his heart.

After his convalescence, Ignatius took to his conversion with vigor. He set out on pilgrimage to Jerusalem, a common penitential practice in those days. On his way, he stopped at the shrine of Our Lady at Montserrat. There, through the grace of confession, he made the definitive choice to put aside his sword and his "knight life" once and for all and adopt a life of poverty, fasting, and penance, just as did the saints he had read about. Under the motto *Ad majoram Dei gloriam* ["For the greater glory of God"], Ignatius would go on to found a religious order known as the Society of Jesus, more commonly referred to as the Jesuits. The Jesuits would become instrumental in combatting heresies and later in spreading the gospel message around the world.

Tools of Discernment

Thanks to their founder, the Jesuits have a well-earned reputation as excellent spiritual directors and practitioners of discernment. The Spiritual Exercises (or simply the Exercises) of Ignatius have helped Catholics for over five centuries discern God's will in their lives. The Exercises are the result of the saint's own journaled reflections on his lived experience, beginning with his convalescence—when he first experienced his heart moving from knighthood to a new goal for his life.

The Exercises consist of four weeks of teachings that are designed to inspire people to make a fundamental choice to follow Christ. These "weeks," however, are not literally seven days in length; they're more like general periods of time.

- Week one focuses on God's love for us and how, even though we've failed to respond to his love at times, God wants to take away our sins and draw us closer to himself.

- Week two focuses on how we are to follow Christ as his disciples.
- Week three focuses on how the Last Supper and Jesus' suffering and death point to God's great love for us.
- Week four focuses on the resurrection, the appearances of Jesus to his disciples, and discernment regarding how we might serve God.

These weeks are rooted in what Ignatius refers to as the First Principle and Foundation: namely, that God created us to know, love, and serve him and that when we respond to God in these ways (knowing, loving, and serving), we discover profound happiness, fulfillment, and ultimately our salvation. Always the pragmatist, Ignatius viewed life as full of choices that would either help you or harm you. The key is discerning which choices will ultimately be helpful.

The fundamental question for those engaged in "the Weeks" or any kind of spiritual discernment is whether or not they *want* to choose that which helps them respond to God more fully. Ignatius' point is obvious: if you believe that God created you and loves you and has given you life—so that you might respond to his love and in turn be fulfilled and happy—you'd be crazy not to choose the paths that lead you closer to God.

Ignatius was also pragmatic about discernment. Discernment, he believed, should be prayerful but should also incorporate our reason and our emotions. Specifically, Ignatius wanted his followers to pay attention to the movement of their thoughts and feelings as they discerned a course of action, especially as they searched for God's will. Peaceful feelings and thoughts that come with discernment are good signs that we are discerning correctly. Peace is a fruit of the Spirit. It can only come from God.

Ignatius described such feelings and thoughts as signs of *consolation*. Conversely, when our spirit is weighed down or depressed, when we are anxious or fearful, these are signs of spiritual *desolation*. Such experiences can make discerning God's will very difficult. If possible, it is best to discern during a time of consolation rather than desolation.

Ignatius also identified the importance of life context in the discernment process. We don't discern things, much less God's will, in a vacuum. We discern in real time and in real life, in which forces, influences, and changes abound. Think about it: if you are experiencing chaos and confusion, or if life is simply hectic or frustrating, how much harder it is to hear the voice of God and follow it. Likewise, when the noise of life lessens a bit, God's "voice" is easier to hear.

By having to discern God's will at different points in his life, beginning with his convalescence, Ignatius became a master of spiritual discernment. His Exercises have been a valuable tool for many Catholics over the centuries. It's incredible to think that if that cannonball had missed his leg, the world would have missed out on a treasure trove of wisdom.

A Seminarian Discerns God's Will

Every summer Creighton University's Institute of Priestly Formation teaches seminarians from around the country about

Ignatian discernment. One of my friends attended the program a number of years back, and what he had to say about it left a lasting impression on me. He began by telling me that part of the formation program included a class on Christian prayer and discernment. The instructor, he recalled, was an Australian Jesuit with an enjoyable accent and a contagious optimism. He introduced the students to the Spiritual Exercises of Ignatius.

When outlining week one of the Exercises—focusing on God's love and choosing to respond to it—the instructor invited the students to close their eyes and imagine Jesus standing before them. Next he asked the students to imagine how Jesus was looking at them, what he was saying, and how he was interacting with them.

This sort of imaginative exercise was also part of Ignatius' approach to Scripture study and reflection. He often encouraged his followers to imagine themselves into the biblical account—for example, mentally placing themselves in the boat with Jesus, who is asleep during the storm—and to pay attention to how they feel and where their thoughts go as the story unfolds.

But back to my friend. As he and the other students opened their eyes, the instructor invited them to share their imaginings. My friend shared how he had imagined Jesus looking rather disappointed. The instructor responded by asking him how his life was going, while cautioning him not to share too much detail. (It was a class, after all, not a counseling session.) The instructor was looking for signs of consolation or desolation in my friend's life.

My friend's life at the time was indeed desolate. He was struggling with panic attacks that he thought were the result of his growing belief that he was unworthy to be a priest. When I asked him why he had believed such a thing, he said he had always imagined God to be like his father, who was never pleased no matter how hard my friend tried. So in the course of seminary training, whenever my friend thought about his faults and sins, all he could imagine was a disappointed God looking back at him.

The summer formation program couldn't have come at a better time for my friend. As he recalls it, the pivotal moment came when the instructor had the students close their eyes, place their index finger on their radial pulse, and imagine that each beat of their heart was God saying to them, "I love you! I love you!" After they opened their eyes again, my friend told the class that he had struggled for most of his life to believe that God really loved him—that he didn't have to try to earn God's love, which of course nobody could do.

The instructor reminded my friend that God created him to know, love, and serve God, so that he could be happy and fulfilled. "God desires our happiness," the instructor said. "Sins don't make God unhappy; they make *us* unhappy. Sins aren't a problem for God. They are a problem for us!"

At that moment, and for the first time in his life, my friend opened his heart to the possibility that he didn't have to be perfect in order to be a priest. He just had to try to let God love him and to return that love the best way he could.

After this experience, my friend discerned that the anxiety he had been feeling for so long wasn't from God, and it wasn't a sign that he should leave the seminary. God didn't want him to be anxious or fearful; God wanted him to be healed and whole. My friend went on to be ordained a diocesan priest. He is still serving as a priest today, and he is also a pretty popular spiritual director. At least, that's what he says!

St. Ignatius was a spiritual master of discernment whose Spiritual Exercises have helped many discover God's will in their lives. For my friend, they were a reminder that he was a beloved child of God and that God delights in removing the obstacles that keep us from loving him in return. Again, sin is not a problem for God; it's a problem for us.

FOR REFLECTION

1. Have you had to make big decisions during a time of desolation? What was the outcome? How about during a time of consolation? How does your faith factor into your decision making?

2. Have you ever had the experience of being sure about the direction of your life only to have something happen that made you rethink everything? How did you navigate that? Was prayer involved?

3. Imagine that Jesus is in the room with you right now. How does he look at you? What does he say? How do the two of you interact with each other?

FOR PRAYER

Lord, help me discern your will for my life, especially when I struggle to see a clear path ahead. When I am faced with a decision, help me consider what will enable me to respond to your love more fully and thus give you greater glory. Doing your will, I know, will lead me to happiness, fulfillment, and salvation. Amen.

CHAPTER 9

St. Thérèse of Lisieux

Seeing Our Personal
Call to Holiness

In our Catholic imagination, we often associate holiness with extremes. When we think of holy people, we think of those whose faith led them to do extraordinary things—the martyrs, miracle workers, and mystics. In other words, people who have lived radical lives for the sake of the gospel message. While such examples of holiness are inspiring, it's hard for us ordinary folks to relate to them.

The truth is that holiness comes in all shapes and sizes. How we express it is unique to the individual person. We see this truth in the life of St. Thérèse of Lisieux.

Thérèse never saw herself living up to the saintly standards of the martyrs and mystics she so admired. In fact, she didn't see herself as having any exceptional gifts at all. But God gradually opened Thérèse's eyes to see that she had her own personal call to holiness. God called her to be *love* and to love people in her own special way.

Longing for God

Born Marie Françoise Thérèse Martin in 1873 in the French town of Alençon, Thérèse was the youngest of five sisters. The Martins were a middle-class family, content to stay in their lane as the French Revolution reshaped their country.

Perhaps because she was the baby of the family, Thérèse was stubborn, entitled, and overly sensitive. Her father, Louis, often referred to her as his "Little Queen." In her autobiography, she admits that she was a rather lazy child, one quite accustomed to getting her own way.

This early experience of privileged life was cut short by the intense suffering and grief that plagued most of her childhood years and followed her into the Carmelite monastery. Her suffering began when she was only four years old and her mother, Zélie, died after a long struggle with cancer. Thérèse's grief manifested itself in periods of physical illness and despondency. From age four to fourteen, she endured spiritual darkness and physical torment, suffering from frequent headaches, insomnia, and a terrible case of religious scruples—an anxiety about the possibility of having sinned.

To help Thérèse cope, Louis took her on frequent trips to church, where they prayed and together adored the Eucharist. Not surprisingly, Louis' fatherly care helped lay the foundation for how Thérèse related to God for the rest of her life. As with each of his daughters, Louis loved Thérèse in a personal way. The love she saw in her father's eyes led her to believe not only that God loved her personally but that she might return his love in her own way. She just needed to figure out what that way was.

(Incidentally, both Louis and Zélie Martin were canonized by Pope Francis on October 18, 2015. Louis was named a patron of mental illnesses, and both Louis and Zélie are patron saints of the domestic church.)

During this period of Thérèse's suffering, the Martin family moved to Lisieux in order to be closer to relatives. Over the span of a few years, three of Thérèse's four older sisters left to enter religious life. Thérèse remained at home with her older sister, Céline, until Céline too entered the convent. Then it was just Thérèse and her father, both still dealing with grief.

Thérèse was determined to enter the convent as well, and she began her quest at an early age. Women were typically admitted to religious life around the age of twenty-one, but for Thérèse, this simply wouldn't do. She wanted to enter the Carmelite monastery at fifteen. Perhaps this was her way of proving to herself that she was in fact uniquely called by God. Regardless, Thérèse knew she could count on the support of her father.

Shortly after her fourteenth birthday, Louis took Thérèse and Céline on a pilgrimage to Rome, hoping that God would reward their act of faith and grant Thérèse her wish to enter the Carmelite community. While on this pilgrimage, Thérèse had the opportunity to participate in an audience with Pope Leo XIII. Determined that nothing would stop her from entering religious life, Thérèse knelt before the pope and cried, pleading with him to let her enter the monastery that same year. Surprised by her ardent desire and her youth, the pope told her that she would enter the following year if God willed it.

And God did will it. Thérèse entered the Carmelite community when she was fifteen. Incidentally, there is no official record of Pope Leo intervening on Thérèse's behalf. But perhaps he pulled a few "papal strings" for her.

And so each of the Martin sisters entered religious life. Léonie, after some false starts, became a Visitation sister, and Marie, Pauline, Céline, and Thérèse became Carmelites. In spite of the restrictions at Carmel, in some ways having so many family members in the same monastery made for a kind of perpetual family reunion.

Thérèse's Little Way

In the monastery, Thérèse's daily routine was very domestic. She worked in the sacristy, cleaned the dining room, wrote poems, and pretty much kept to herself. Her fellow nuns found her kind and competent, but by all outward appearances, there was nothing extraordinary about her. This might lead us to conclude that Thérèse's determination to be outstanding in God's eyes had faded. The truth, however, is that her desire to be special was being purified.

As a religious, Thérèse often compared herself to the saints she read about, and she found herself lacking the gifts and virtues they had. She was quick to note who and what she was not. While she admired the martyrs, she knew she wasn't called to be one. Though she was impressed by the mystics and their extraordinary intimacy and insight, she knew that wasn't her calling either.

One day, as she was thinking about how she could best serve God, Thérèse began reading chapter twelve of St. Paul's First Letter to the Corinthians. This chapter speaks of the various members of the Church—apostles, prophets, teachers—and how their gifts build up the body of Christ. Recognizing that she wasn't an apostle, a prophet, or a teacher, that she wasn't someone in the Church worthy of note, caused Thérèse some grief. But this grief was only momentary.

As Thérèse describes in her autobiography, *The Story of a Soul,* after reflecting on St. Paul's teaching, she felt as if her eyes were directed to—her actual words were that they "fell upon"—another teaching of St. Paul just a few verses later. He points out the way that is more excellent than any other, the way of love (see 1 Corinthians 12:31). From there, of course, he launches into his famous hymn to love, which begins, "If I speak in human and angelic tongues but do not have love, I am a resounding gong or a clashing cymbal" (1 Corinthians 13:1).

It was at this moment that Thérèse realized her path to holiness. She was called to be *love*—to love God and others to the best of *her* ability and in *her* own way. This would later be referred to as Thérèse's *little way*.

Thérèse's little way began in discovering her call to be love in the broader world, which in her enclosed circumstances took the form of intercessory prayer. Thérèse delighted at the thought of being an intercessor for others, begging God on their behalf for his love and mercy.

Having found her calling, Thérèse thought about holiness differently. It was no longer about extreme sacrifices or supernatural abilities, and it was not about having certain gifts and abilities. It was about loving and being loved. Loving God in her own personal way, she realized, delighted his divine heart.

As Thérèse looked for analogies to refine and explain her little way, she imagined creation as a garden and humanity composed of countless individual flowers. Though she was partial to roses, she humbly recognized that not everyone could be a rose, nor should they want to be. God, she believed, didn't want a garden of roses. He wanted a garden of diverse flowers, each growing according to his unique design. For Thérèse, this diversity was proof of God's wisdom and greatness.

Another foundational tenet of Thérèse's little way was her unshakable belief that when we humble ourselves, God will elevate us. Reflecting on the mountaintop as a prominent image of spiritual perfection—one that is peppered throughout the Bible—Thérèse couldn't imagine herself having the strength or courage to scale the mountain. Such a feat was far too demanding for her. In her autobiography, she comments on how she desperately searched the Scriptures for some kind of "elevator" that would take her to the top of the mountain of spiritual perfection, so that she wouldn't have to make the climb! While some may associate such a perspective with spiritual laziness, in Thérèse it was a profound act of humility.

Having concluded that there wasn't any extraordinary thing she could do for God, Thérèse committed herself to doing all things—even domestic, seemingly inconsequential things—with great love. Humility was the source and motivation for everything Thérèse would do as she journeyed along her little way. Her childlike trust in God's grace and his unique love for her would be her guide. Together these roots of *humility* and *trust* produced a beautiful "little flower" in God's garden. And Thérèse has become known as the Little Flower.

While Thérèse's role as an earthly intercessor didn't last very long, she hoped to spend eternity interceding for others. She intended to shower people with roses as a sign of their answered prayers and of God's love for them. Upon her death the fragrance of roses became apparent to all who were present. And today when people pray for Thérèse's intercession and their prayers are answered, they sometimes receive confirmation through the sign of a rose—either seeing or receiving a rose or suddenly smelling roses when none are present.

Perhaps by this sign Thérèse is teaching us a final lesson in her *little way:* those who wish to become flowers in God's garden need only recognize the beauty of who they are and choose to grow where they are planted. When we see ourselves as God sees us, we discover and embrace the beauty that is always there inside, hidden in our ordinariness.

Thirteen years after her death, the Church had Thérèse's body exhumed as part of the canonization process, the Church's official process for declaring a person a saint. Onlookers were amazed to see that, although her body was in a naturally decayed state, resting on her bones was the palm branch that was placed in her coffin during her burial. It was still fresh and green!

A Mother Who Loves in Her Own Little Way

God helped St. Thérèse see that she was called to holiness in her own way. She was called to be *love* in the world in a way that only she could demonstrate. When it came to spiritual perfection, she preferred elevators to mountain climbing, being raised up by God's love rather than straining for it. Thérèse's *little way* is a model for each of us in discovering our own path to holiness.

Many of us think of our mothers as saints. I'm no different. And like so many mothers, my mother, Paula, would be the first to tell you that she's no saint.

As with Thérèse, God invited my mother to discover her call to holiness within community life. Hers is not a religious community but rather the domestic church of the Halbach family. My mother began her "novitiate" in our community at the early age of eighteen. But unlike Thérèse, she did not require papal approval to do so!

My mom's holiness is obvious to me; I've been the beneficiary of her "little way" my entire life. She follows her vocation to be love by telling me she loves me in her own unique way. My mother has never considered herself a wordsmith, and she often shies away from saying too much about how she really feels (except when it comes to politics). But whenever a birthday or holiday rolls around, Mom proves herself to be the beautiful little flower she is.

First, she spends a ridiculous amount of time looking for the right card for me. Incidentally, I've been with her when she was picking out cards; it is really something to behold.

She'll read a card, look at it, read it again, and either hold onto it or put it back. This is but the first round of her draft picks. There is also a quarter and semifinal round. Once a winning card has emerged—one that says exactly what she wants to say—she goes home and begins a second phase of scrutiny: the underlining.

My mother decides which words are worthy of note and then underlines these "chosen ones." I have come to understand that the underlined words are of great significance. If I don't articulate them with emphasis as I read the card to all those gathered, I know I have somehow let Mom down. (Incidentally, my mother tends to highlight almost every word of the card, leaving out only a few articles like "a" and "the" and the occasional preposition.)

As silly as all this may seem, I have found this little gesture so endearing. Coming from a woman who doesn't believe herself gifted enough to express her feelings in her own words, it's as if the underlines speak her language of love to me. Truly, I am amazed at how clearly my mom can communicate her love for me without saying anything at all—though she does in fact take the time to also tell me she loves me.

In addition to the sacred speech of underlines, another little way my mother communicates her love for me is by drawing a little heart on the card. Regrettably, the significance of the heart was lost on me for some time, until one Christmas my mom forgot to mark my card with a heart but remembered to put one on my brother's card. "What a tragic injustice!" I thought. I turned to my mom and asked, somewhat tongue-in-cheek, "Do you love Todd more than me?" We all had a laugh, and then Mom grabbed a pen and drew a heart on my card and made everything all right again. Justice was restored.

Like Thérèse, my mother doesn't see herself as having extraordinary gifts; she definitely doesn't see herself as a saint. But my mother knows how to be love in her own unique way. Her card giving and underlining are legendary in the Halbach family. Then there are many unique and "little" ways she tells us how much she loves us.

I can't imagine anyone, even Shakespeare, saying, "I love you," any more eloquently than Mom does. The card's words, "A rose by any other name would smell as sweet," are true and fitting.[11] In her own way, my mom is a rose in God's garden.

FOR REFLECTION

1. It's often said that *comparison is the thief of joy.* Do you compare yourself to others? How does that leave you feeling?

2. How have you thought about holiness in the past? What did you think it looked like? Has your perception changed, based on the insights of St. Thérèse?

3. As you reflect on St. Thérèse's *little way,* what things do you see yourself already doing to offer God's love to others? What traits do you have that lend themselves to sharing God's love?

FOR PRAYER

Lord, help me see how you are calling me to be holy in a personal way, as only I can be. Open my eyes to the gifts and talents you have given me to be love in the world, and give me the courage to believe that I am called to be a saint. Amen.

CHAPTER 10

St. Faustina Kowalska

Seeing God's
Lavish Mercy

I f you distill the Bible down to its most essential element, *mercy* is what remains. The mercy of God, in Jesus Christ, is the core of the good news. The Son is the very incarnation of mercy; and the Spirit leads the Church ever onward in the mission of sharing God's mercy through word and sacrament.

The visions of St. Faustina Kowalska reveal the lavish mercy of God in Jesus Christ. Through them and the Divine Mercy image and chaplet they inspired, Catholics are encouraged to trust in Christ's mercy, especially at the hour of their death.

Jesus' Call

Born on August 25, 1905, in Glogowiec, Poland, Helena Kowalska was the third of ten children. The Kowalskas struggled financially; the father, Stanislaw, had a difficult time finding work as a carpenter. Though not materially blessed, the Kowalskas were spiritually blessed in Faustina, who would eventually make her family name a permanent part of the Catholic spiritual tradition.

Helena began to receive spiritual blessings at a very early age. At seven, she was inspired to enter religious life—an inspiration that she attributed to time spent in Eucharistic adoration. Helena eventually became a religious but not without some resistance from her parents. Stanislaw and Marianna were not anti-religious by any means; reports of Helena's early life suggest that they were ardent practitioners of the faith. Their specific resistance to Helena's religious vocation is unclear.

In many accounts of the lives of the saints, there is a pivotal moment when the saint decides to follow Christ. For Helena that moment came at the age of nineteen. She and her sister, Natalia, were attending a local dance when Helena had a vision of Jesus. He said to her, "How long shall I put up with you and how long will you keep putting Me off?"[12]

Immediately after the vision ceased, Helena left the dance and went to the local cathedral seeking guidance. While praying, she heard Jesus tell her to enter a convent. So Helena went home, packed her things, and left for Warsaw without her parents' permission. Once there, she entered the first church she saw. (There are a lot of Catholic churches in Poland, by the way. It wouldn't have taken long to spot one.) She told the pastor that God was calling her to the religious life. He sent her to stay with a Mrs. Lipszycowa until she found a convent that would accept her.

Helena's poverty was an obstacle to her acceptance, and several convents turned her away. (Even today religious communities and seminaries have rules regarding the financial situation of candidates. For example, there are regulations regarding the reception of a candidate who is burdened with financial debt.) Helena was eventually accepted by the Congregation of the Sisters of Our Lady of Mercy, on the condition that she pay for her own religious habit. Helena worked as a housemaid for almost a year to earn enough money.

On April 30, 1926, Helena entered the novitiate under the name Sr. Maria Faustina of the Blessed Sacrament. To all appearances, Sr. Faustina was rather ordinary; there was nothing to set her apart from the other sisters. She obeyed the rule and did her work.

Visited by Mercy

In 1930 Sr. Faustina became sick with what was later thought to be tuberculosis. She convalesced for a few months at a farm owned by the convent. There she began to receive private revelations in which she saw Jesus. He instructed her to paint what she saw and to include, as a signature, the words "Jesus, I trust in You."

Faustina procured an artist and relayed her vision to him. The Divine Mercy image, as it would come to be called, depicts Jesus risen from the dead, with wounded hands—one raised in blessing and the other touching his heart, from which emanate red and white rays. These rays symbolize the blood and water that flowed from his heart after it was pierced by the soldier's lance. The red ray also signifies the life of souls, and the white signifies the water that makes souls righteous—that is, the waters of Baptism.

In subsequent visions, Faustina saw an angel of God sent to destroy a certain city. She prayed that God would spare the city, but her prayers were initially ineffective. It was then that the Holy Trinity appeared to her, inspiring her to pray the following words:

> Eternal Father, I offer You the Body and Blood, Soul and Divinity of Your dearly beloved Son, Our Lord Jesus Christ, for our sins and those of the whole world; for the sake of His sorrowful Passion, have mercy on us.[13]

When Faustina prayed these words, the angel withdrew from the city. Faustina continued to pray the prayer, and in a later vision, Jesus revealed to her that the prayer should end with the words "and on the whole world." This helped Faustina understand that the prayer—which Jesus described as a "chaplet"—was not just for her but for all humanity.

This prayer of petition and praise has come to be known as the Divine Mercy Chaplet. People usually pray it on the beads of a rosary and often at 3:00 p.m., the "hour of mercy," because that is thought to be the hour Jesus died on the cross (see Luke 23:44).

The chaplet is a graced prayer. Jesus promised Faustina that anyone who prays the chaplet will receive his mercy at the hour of their death: "I will stand between My Father and the dying person, not as the just Judge but as the merciful

Savior."[14] Because of Faustina and her visions, the Divine
Mercy image and chaplet have become popular devotions
among Catholics today.

The Scandal of God's Mercy and Faustina's Diary

As much as mercy signifies blessing and gift, reconciliation
and reunion, our perceptions about who should receive God's
mercy and about how much mercy is too much can conjure
up anger and judgmentalism—things that are divisive and
absolutely opposed to mercy. The parables of the prodigal
son and the laborers in the vineyard (see Luke 15:11-32; Matthew 20:1-16) teach us that mercy has nothing to do with
fairness as we humans understand it. Nevertheless, when we
see the mercy of God at work in the lives of others—particularly those we don't care for or those who have harmed
us—we can be scandalized. We presume to judge God on
how he should dispense his mercy! Only in Jesus do we find
a harmony between the concept of judgment and the truth of
mercy, a harmony that Faustina's diary helps reveal.

Inspired by her spiritual directors, Faustina recorded her
visions, which were later compiled and published as *Divine
Mercy in My Soul: The Diary of Saint Maria Faustina Kowalska*. As with all things having to do with God's mercy, Faustina's
diary inspired hope as well as criticism. The latter was due
mostly to grammatical errors and omissions in the translation from Faustina's native Polish to Italian. But some in the
Church also looked on the diary with suspicion because of its
radical claims about God's mercy.

For example, in one vision, Faustina reports that Jesus said: "The greater the sinner, the greater the right he has to My Mercy."[15] At first glance, to suggest that sinners have a *right* to God's mercy seems absurd. No creature has rights over its Creator. The rights we enjoy—the rights that pertain to our freedom and dignity, for example—flow from God. It is not surprising, therefore, that this particular vision of Faustina was initially perceived by the Church as borderline heretical.

In response to these criticisms, Pope Pius XII, in 1958, placed the *Diary* on the Vatican's Index of Prohibited Books (*Index Librorum Prohibitorum*). But the *Diary* didn't remain there. Roughly twenty years later, Pope John Paul II removed it from the Index, having ensured that its corrected Italian translation was free of errors. The debate around a sinner's right to God's mercy was also put to rest. Although God is not subordinate to humanity, God can choose to become the servant of humanity and therefore allow himself to be beholden to it—a central theme of Paul's Letter to the Philippians (see Philippians 2:5-11).

Mercy is the core of the gospel message. The *Diary*, along with the Divine Mercy image and the Chaplet of Divine Mercy, has helped keep God's mercy at the center of Catholic spirituality, worship, and life. They give hope especially to the dying, who will soon stand before the judgement seat of God.

Mercy Can Set Us Free

One of the best examples of dealing with the scandal of God's mercy comes from a woman I knew in a former parish. Her decision to extend God's mercy—and to refuse to sit in judgment—made all the difference in her life and set her free.

This woman—we'll call her Sharon—had been a long-time practicing Catholic, married for several years, with two kids. One day, out of the blue, her husband confessed to her that he had been unfaithful. Making an already bad situation worse, the person he had an affair with was her best friend; we'll call her Bridget. Upon hearing the terrible news, Sharon became confused and angry. Her husband, in turn, moved out of their house, leaving Sharon alone with her grief and the responsibility of raising their children.

Bridget was a member of Sharon's congregation, so for the next two years, Sharon chose not to attend church. She couldn't bear the thought of seeing Bridget there. When I asked Sharon what those years were like for her, she told me that she didn't remember much except the anger that she felt toward her ex-husband and Bridget. It consumed her.

Every day Sharon's mind wrestled with the same questions: How could Bridget betray me? How could my husband cheat on me? Am I not a good wife? What's wrong with me? But there were no answers. Of one thing Sharon was sure: she wanted God to bring down his judgment on both her ex-husband and Bridget.

Eventually Sharon grew tired of letting her anger and her embarrassment determine her choices. She would go back to church even though Bridget might be there. It was her church too, after all! Providentially, the day that Sharon made this momentous decision happened to be Divine Mercy Sunday, though at the time she didn't know it.

Sharon was inspired by the Mass, especially the homily, which focused on how God's mercy can set us free. After the dismissal, she decided to go over to Bridget and talk to her. She described this as nearly an out-of-body experience. She felt she was being compelled to meet with Bridget.

Before Sharon could speak, Bridget broke out in a tearful apology and threw her arms around Sharon. Seeing the contrition on Bridget's face brought Sharon to tears also. She found herself forgiving Bridget for her betrayal.

When I asked Sharon why she decided to forgive Bridget, she said that first she forgave Bridget because the anger and the bitterness she had been carrying around was too much to bear. It was ruining her health and her life. Second, in that moment, Sharon thought about what the situation must have been like for Bridget, who had been her friend for many years. Sharon realized, in those few moments of tearful hugging, that if she were Bridget, she would need to be forgiven in order to move on with life.

Sharon and Bridget never reestablished their friendship. But having encountered the mercy of God, both women experienced a renewed sense of freedom and worth.

FOR REFLECTION

1. Do you believe that God can forgive you for your sins? If so, where do you most need God's mercy in your life? How can you start to forgive yourself and approach God for his forgiveness?

2. Consider times when you've had to forgive someone. Were you able to do it? What was that like? Are you better for it? Is the other person better for it?

3. Does the Divine Mercy message speak to your life? Do you find it encouraging, or does the lavishness of God's mercy make you uncomfortable? What can you do to show God's mercy to others?

FOR PRAYER

Lord, I always stand in need of your mercy, even when things seem fine. Your mercy not only forgives sins but also opens new pathways for blessing. Help me be more merciful toward myself and others, for your glory. Amen.

CHAPTER 11

St. Teresa of Calcutta

Seeing Light
in the Darkness

At times life can lead us into some pretty dark places: for example, when we face the death of a loved one, a divorce, a job loss, or an unfortunate diagnosis. Mental health issues too can darken our outlook on life and lead us into unhealthy, even unholy behaviors and relationships.

Running in tandem with life, our spiritual journeys can become quite dark at times: when our prayers appear to go unanswered, when we wait on a miracle that doesn't come, or when someone representing the faith lets us down. In these moments, our faith can wane, even to a point where God seems to have abandoned us.

Mother Teresa was no stranger to spiritual darkness or the darkness of human misery. Her time as the Saint of Calcutta—caring for the poor, the sick, and the dying—was a daily crucible. Her only light during this period of her life, which stretched over fifty years, was her faith in God and her love for the crucified Jesus. Her union with the suffering Christ enabled her, as she put it, to enter into the "dark holes" of the lives of the marginalized, the forgotten, and the suffering ones she encountered. This redemptive darkness Mother Teresa embraced became the very portal through which the light of Christ's resurrection shone on all those to whom she ministered.

Called to Be Light

Born on August 26, 1910, in what is now the capital of North Macedonia, Anjezë Gonxha Bojaxhiu always felt a strong religious calling. She described herself as having a thirst for souls from a very young age. She eventually joined a missionary order in Ireland, the Sisters of Loreto. There she chose the name Teresa, after St. Thérèse of Lisieux, a patron saint of missionaries.

In 1929 Sr. Teresa joined the Loreto community in Calcutta, India, and for twenty years she worked as a teacher at the St. Mary's School for Girls. One day, on the way from Calcutta to a much-anticipated retreat in Darjeeling, Teresa had an inspiration that she referred to as "a call within a call." She was filled with the sense of Jesus' thirst for souls—an interpretation she later applied to Jesus' words from the cross, "I thirst" (John 19:28).

Following a series of interior locutions and visions over the next few months, Teresa came to believe that Jesus was calling her to be his light and to radiate his love on souls. Specifically, she believed God was asking her to establish a new religious community in Calcutta—the order now known as the Missionaries of Charity—dedicated to serving the poorest of the poor and the most neglected. The order was officially founded in 1950. Mother Teresa later established the Missionaries of Charity Brothers, a contemplative order, along with the Missionaries of Charity Fathers and some lay-led apostolates, such as the Co-Workers of Mother Teresa and the Lay Missionaries of Charity.

Mother Teresa was known for her generosity, kindness, and smile. Not even her closest companions knew that she struggled with spiritual darkness—she referred to it simply as "the darkness"—for the nearly fifty years that followed her call on the way to Darjeeling. Her darkness became public knowledge with the publication in 2009 of *Come Be My Light: The Private Writings of the Saint of Calcutta*.[16]

In part this darkness was a sharing in the poverty of the poorest of the poor, the result of empathizing with those she served. Teresa wasn't one to distance herself from the sick and the dying she treated. She wanted to accompany them all the way, holding nothing back. She described this type of care as the work of entering into peoples' "dark holes."

Teresa's *little way* of love—a phrase she adopted from her patron saint, Thérèse of Lisieux—was a kind of spiritual sharing of light and darkness. The person Mother Teresa was caring for would share their darkness with her, and she in turn would share her light. It was the light of faith, which she kept burning brightly, fueled by the love of Christ for her personally and by his thirst for all souls. Heroically, she allowed herself to enter into the darkness of the poorest of the poor even though she experienced none of the consolations of the faith she brought to them through her service.

At some point, as the darkness persisted, Teresa realized she needed someone to confide in, someone who could enter into the "dark holes" of her life and help her understand why God allowed her to feel so abandoned and alone, despite her faith that God was near. She found this companionship in her bishop, her spiritual directors, and her confessor. They were like little lights for her, helping illuminate what became a long journey through the darkness. Through their companionship, Teresa realized that her experiences of loneliness and emptiness were actually graces from God. These experiences helped her enter more fully into the suffering of the poor, into the suffering of Christ on the cross, and into his thirst for souls.

Mother Teresa came to see her self-described nothingness as the very quality that made her a useful instrument in God's hands. In other words, less room for Teresa meant more room for God. Nothingness—especially as manifest in her sense of abandonment—was her call to complete diminishment of her ego. It was, she said, how God made room in her soul for his infinite love.

Mother Teresa and her missionaries' empathic care included provision of the basic necessities of life—warmth, comfort, encouragement, and love. Their service gave the poor, the sick, and the dying of Calcutta the opportunity to experience Christ's saving love in this world before they passed on to the next. By choosing to embrace the cross of Christ and to spiritually share in his passion, Mother Teresa and her missionaries brought light into the dark holes of countless people.

Wounds that Heal

My friend—we'll call him Bill—spent years praying and sharing his faith with patients in hospitals and hospices. He certainly saw a lot of suffering and death. Intrigued and inspired by Bill, I decided to meet with him over coffee and ask him what those years were like for him.

Bill simply smiled, sipped his coffee, and said with great sincerity, "You know, those were the best years of my life." Then I asked him why he felt called to care for the sick and the dying, as I couldn't imagine the toll it must have taken on him. He said some things that surprised me.

At first Bill didn't know why he was in that particular ministry. He felt unprepared for it, out of place, not spiritually qualified. But after a while, he came to realize that God had *chosen* him. "And you don't say no to God!" he said with a laugh.

I asked Bill how he knew he was chosen. He said that he had discovered his unique calling by what he saw transpire between him and the patients. He began to observe how his personal woundedness made him more accessible and more empathetic to the sufferings of others. In a way that only God can make possible, that woundedness authenticated the sincerity of his ministry, helping others accept the truth of the gospel message more readily and more completely.

As we talked, Bill's thoughts turned to one patient in particular: a woman dying of cancer. Bill passed by her hospital room every day, and he noticed that she never seemed to have any visitors. Determined that no one would be lonely on his watch, he decided to enter her room.

The woman grimaced as he entered, and Bill knew he wasn't welcome. Nevertheless, he introduced himself and offered to stay and watch television with her if she'd like. The woman quickly declined his offer and told him to "get the hell" out of her room.

Instead of leaving, Bill said with a cheeky smile, "I'd like to see you make me leave. I might be old, but you are stuck in bed, dying, which gives me the upper hand here." This, he said, made the woman smile and helped put her at ease.

The two of them talked for some time that day. Bill learned that in fact the woman had relatives in the area, but no one came to visit her—an unfortunate result of her years of alcoholism and general moodiness. Bill shared that he too had struggled with alcohol, that it was a predisposition he had inherited from his father.

Bill talked candidly and at length about how alcohol had taken over his life and strained his relationships with his family and friends. He told the woman that he had been sober for ten years, thanks to a friend who was a recovering alcoholic. His friend had invited him into the AA program and accompanied him through it.

As we sipped our coffee that day, Bill laughed and said to me, "You know, if it wasn't for my friend sharing with me his own struggles with alcoholism, I wouldn't have believed his recovery was real."

Reflecting again on the woman in the hospital, Bill said that sharing his past with her helped her gradually open up to him and trust him. So when he told her that she was good and that God still loved her very much, she believed him. This was a lesson that he had learned as part of his recovery.

"She wasn't Catholic," Bill said, as he recalled the woman's final day on earth, "so she wasn't interested in any sacramental reconciliation. But she did want to tell God she was sorry for the mistakes she had made."

She ended up disclosing to Bill the darkness she had been carrying around with her for years—the lies she told and the anger she unleashed on her family. Bill entered into this dark hole of her life. They prayed together for God's mercy, and they prayed that she would place her trust in his love for her as she passed from this life.

When they had finished sharing and praying, the woman told Bill that, until she met him, she had planned on taking her sins to her grave. But she found him to be disarming and nonjudgmental, and the fact that he had shared in her struggle with alcohol gave his words greater authority and authenticity. When the woman died later that day, she had a look of peace on her face such that "it was a privilege to be with her and to share in her darkness," Bill said. I could see that it was a darkness he had helped dispel with the light of his faith.

FOR REFLECTION

1. What are the "dark holes" of your life? Do you believe God wants to meet you in those places and share his light and his love with you? How can you open yourself to that possibility?

2. Have you ever encountered a "wounded healer"? What was that person like? Have you ever considered that your own weaknesses and wounds might be sources of healing for others? How might Mother Teresa's example help you embrace that possibility?

3. Can you recall times in your life or the lives of others when God drew light from darkness, goodness from evil? How can this reality help you accompany those who are walking in darkness or trapped in evil, so that they can make their way to the light?

FOR PRAYER

Lord, if I am honest with myself, I know that I have wounds that need healing—physical, psychological, and spiritual wounds. Help me see my wounds as opportunities for grace, not only for myself but for others who suffer. Please bring healing to us all.

Lord, after your resurrection, you kept your wounds and showed them to your apostles. Help my woundedness be a point of connection with others and a sign of your presence and peace. Amen.

CHAPTER 12

Blessed Carlo Acutis

Seeing Today's
Mission Fields

Multiple generations now have grown up with the internet. These so-called "digital natives" often use it as their primary means of communication. I can't tell you how many times I've seen people sitting at a restaurant and texting their friends (or even each other!) as they wait for their food. It's a brave new world—one that requires courageous and thoughtful Catholics who are willing to share the love of Jesus online, because that is where many people are today.

Jesus said to his disciples, "The harvest is plentiful, but the laborers are few" (Luke 10:2, RSVCE). Today the internet offers laborers the potential for a more plentiful harvest than the Church has ever seen. Cyberspace is mission territory.

Blessed Carlo Acutis understood this well. He is a member of the millennial generation—those born between 1983 and

1996—and the first millennial to be beatified by the Catholic Church. He is a shining example of how we can approach the internet as a mission field.

Called to Sainthood

Carlo was born in London on May 3, 1991, but grew up in Milan, Italy, where his family moved shortly after his birth. He enjoyed playing video games, surfing the net, going to movies, and reading comic books; in these ways, he was a typical boy. Where Carlo differed from his peers was in his zeal for Jesus, something he experienced from a very early age.

Often it is faith-filled families that form future saints, but there are exceptions. Take Carlo's parents, Andrea and Antonia, for example. They were good parents but not particularly religious. In an often-cited interview, Antonia revealed that she had only been to church three times before Carlo died: once for her wedding, once for Carlo's First Communion, and once for his Confirmation. The Acutis household, you could say, was not exactly a vibrant domestic church.

Despite this, Carlo, from a very young age, was sensitive to God's grace and to the spiritual life. He had a dream when he was four in which his deceased maternal grandfather appeared to him and asked him for his prayers. After his First Communion, Carlo attended daily Mass and frequently went to confession. He had a hunger for the Eucharist, referring to it as his personal "highway to heaven."

One might wonder where Carlo received his zeal for the faith. The answer, I think, is in the sacraments. Carlo's decision to attend daily Mass was, in effect, a decision to receive God's grace often. More grace leads to a greater abundance of faith and blessing. It's a simple formula, really. The more grace we receive, the more we want to receive, and the more we want to give to others out of the abundance of our abundance.

The saints knew this, and so did Carlo. His life goal was to be more like Jesus. The more he received the Eucharist, the nearer he came to achieving his goal. Staying in communion with Jesus, he believed (and he was right!), would lead him and those around him to happiness and salvation. "To always be united to Jesus," he said, "was the program of my life."[17]

To their credit, Carlo's parents left him free to pursue this goal. They remind me, in a way, of the parents on *Family Ties*, a TV show from the 1980s. The show featured the actor Michael J. Fox, who played the character of Alex, the oldest child of the fictitious Keaton family. For most of the series, Alex was in high school, but he always acted much older than his age. He was politically conservative, read the newspaper every morning, worried about the stock market, and carried a briefcase to school. He was out to conquer the business world.

Alex's parents, Steven and Elyse, hippies of the sixties, were much more liberal politically than Alex. Steven and Elyse couldn't figure out how their son turned out the way he did. They certainly didn't raise him to be the conservative he was, but they loved him and let him be himself. For his part, Alex would often question, tongue-in-cheek, whether he was adopted. The show offers a reminder that sometimes kids know who they want to be and what they want to do from a very early age—and it might be completely different from what parents envision.

Carlo Acutis knew what he wanted. Perhaps Andrea and Antonia were practicing a type of holy parenting. Initially they weren't inclined to get involved in Carlo's quest for holiness, but they didn't prevent him from pursuing faith. They let him ask his questions, pray, and participate in the liturgy.

As in Carlo's case, these holy desires sometimes spring up on their own. When this happens, parents should be grateful and let the Holy Spirit move in the child's life. The time it takes to drive a child to Mass or to religious education might make all the difference in their life years later.

Over time Carlo's witness of faith and love for the Eucharist had a profound effect on Andrea and Antonia, drawing them to faith. Antonia even referred to Carlo as her "little savior."

The Eucharist led Carlo not only into deeper prayer but also into service of others. During his school years, he often befriended kids who were bullied, he volunteered at soup kitchens and homeless shelters, and he became a catechist. He invited friends whose parents were divorcing to hang out at his house, where they could take their minds off the problems at home.

Jesus on the Internet

During his high school years, Carlo developed the aggressive form of leukemia that would claim his life. He was never one to waste time—he restricted his video-game activity to one hour a week, for example—but his illness intensified his desire to spend every remaining minute of life trying to imitate Christ and the saints. With little time remaining, Carlo looked for ways to share his faith with as many people as possible. One way he did that was through prudent use of the internet. Carlo was a gifted programmer who understood the dangers of the internet as well as its potential as a tool for evangelization. He chose not to succumb to the kind of hyper-consumerism and self-obsession that internet marketers and social media influencers offer. Instead, combining his love for the Eucharist with his skills as a programmer, he constructed a website devoted to Eucharistic miracles and to particular saints and their devotion to the Eucharist. The site is active today and managed by the Associazione Amici di Carlo Acutis. It can be accessed at http://www.miracolieucaristici.org/en/liste/list.html.

Pope Francis spoke of Carlo in his 2019 post-synodal exhortation *Christus Vivit* [Christ Lives]:

Carlo was well aware that the whole apparatus of communications, advertising and social networking can be used to lull us, to make us addicted to consumerism and buying the latest thing on the market, obsessed with our free time, caught up in negativity. Yet he knew how to use the new communications technology to transmit the Gospel, to communicate values and beauty.

Carlo didn't fall into the trap. He saw that many young people, wanting to be different, really end up being like everyone else, running after whatever the powerful set before them with the mechanisms of consumerism and distraction. In this way they do not bring forth the gifts the Lord has given them;

they do not offer the world those unique personal talents that God has given to each of them. As a result, Carlo said, "everyone is born as an original, but many people end up dying as photocopies." Don't let that happen to you![18]

Carlo was an evangelizer, both in person and online. While he made use of the internet and other modern technologies, he was not owned by them nor obsessed with them. It was clear to all who knew him that Christ—not the internet or trends or material things—was at the center of Carlo's life.

You can find out more about Carlo at his official site, http://www.carloacutis-en.org.

Becoming an Online Missionary: Disciples 2.0

In previous chapters, I've used this section to highlight an individual who offers a modern example of seeing things in a new way with the help of God. In this chapter, I'd like to offer a few brief thoughts about how to begin sharing your faith using the internet.

For starters, the internet is full of information of all kinds. Some sources are more trustworthy than others. It's important, as you enter this universe and start sharing your faith, that your witness be a reliable one, one that can be trusted. Always strive to be authentic, keeping in mind that your faith witness is wrapped up in your life story; it's part of who you are as a child of God.

The most engaging faith stories are those that speak from personal experience, honestly, in a straightforward manner, without questionable embellishment. And when it comes to sharing your faith online, make sure you are sharing it *your way*, in *your own words*. If you aren't sure that what you are saying is theologically correct—a critical aspect of trustworthiness—find a reliable Catholic site that invites questions, and ask away! Or ask your pastor or another trusted source before you hit "send."

The second point I'd like to make is that if you're going to evangelize online, it's essential that you respect other people's voices. The internet is a crowded space, with people from diverse backgrounds and experiences talking to (and unfortunately often yelling at) each other. Don't talk *at* people, much less yell at them. Try listening to the other person's point of view before responding. A little bit of common courtesy goes a long way.

Finally, keep in mind that when you share your faith online, you don't always have to share a personal story or anecdote. Be creative! Travelers along the internet superhighway have all sorts of tools available to help them create and share content. Maybe instead of a story, you can share a Bible verse. There are plenty of free software programs and social platforms that can help you share your favorite verse in a unique way. Also consider sharing photos and images (always check the copyright!) that you find inspiring. As the saying goes, a picture is worth a thousand words.

You don't have to be a saint to share your faith online. As did Blessed Carlo Acutis, you just have to see the internet as a mission field, as a place where the good news of Christ should be present. Take your cue from Carlo, and don't waste another moment. Take the love of Jesus with you wherever you go, even when you go online.

FOR REFLECTION

1. Are there social media personalities you follow or platforms you use to find images, quotes, and stories that inspire you in your faith? Have you considered sharing content from them through your own social media outlets—by retweets, for example? If you don't use social media, would you consider doing so, even in a limited way?

2. Have you ever thought of yourself as an evangelizer—someone called to share the good news of Jesus with others? The call to share the gospel is a call for all disciples. If you haven't embraced this call, ask the Holy Spirit to help you get started.

3. Do you think that your faith story is worth sharing with others? You might not think so, but perhaps God does. He'll help you identify those points in your story that will touch the hearts of others. Ask God to help you identify a personal experience of faith, and then consider how you can share it with others.

FOR PRAYER

Lord, you said that the harvest is plentiful but the laborers are few. Help me see the internet as a place where I can make your love more visible. Help me discern how I might share my faith with others online, in ways that are respectful, authentic, and joy filled. Amen.

Notes

1. Pope Francis, General Audience, May 17, 2017, https://www.vatican.va/content/francesco/en/audiences/2017/documents/papa-francesco_20170517_udienza-generale.html.
2. Bruce Marshall, *The World, the Flesh and Father Smith* (New York: Houghton Mifflin, 1945), 108.
3. Henry Chadwick, trans., *Saint Augustine Confessions* (London: Oxford University Press, 2008), 3.
4. Chadwick, 145.
5. Chadwick, 153.
6. Chadwick, 201.
7. St. Bonaventure, *The Life of Saint Francis of Assisi,* trans. E. Gurney Salter, chap. 1, no. 3, https://www.ecatholic2000.com/bonaventure/assisi/francis.shtml.
8. Peter Doyle, *Butler's Lives of the Saints: October*, rev. ed. (Collegeville, MN: Liturgical Press, 1996), 18.
9. *Catechism of the Catholic Church*, 159, quoting Vatican I, *Dei Filius* [On the Catholic Faith] 4; Vatican II, *Gaudium et Spes* [The Church in the Modern World] 36.

10. Pope John Paul II, Homily for the Canonization of Juan Diego Cuauhtlatoatzin, July 31, 2002, www.vatican.va/content/john-paul-ii/en/homilies/2002/documents/hf_jp-ii_hom_20020731_canonization-mexico.html.

11. William Shakespeare, *Romeo and Juliet,* act 2, scene 1.

12. *Divine Mercy in My Soul: Diary of Saint Maria Faustina Kowalska* (Stockbridge, MA: Marian Press, 2005), §9.

13. *Divine Mercy in My Soul,* §475.

14. *Divine Mercy in My Soul,* §1541.

15. *Divine Mercy in My Soul,* §723.

16. Mother Teresa, *Come Be My Light: The Private Writings of the Saint of Calcutta,* ed. Brian Kolodiejchuk (New York: Doubleday, 2007).

17. Nicola Gori, *Carlo Acutis: The First Millenial Saint* (Huntington, IN: Our Sunday Visitor, 2021), 1.

18. Pope Francis, *Christus Vivit* [Christ Lives], Post-Synodal Apostolic Exhortation to Young People, March 25, 2019, 105–106, www.vatican.va/content/francesco/en/apost_exhortations/documents/papa-francesco_esortazione-ap_20190325_christus-vivit.html.